Advance praise for *The Spirit of Saint Francis*

Francis our pope is revealing through his daily life what Jesus announced and the way he lived. This little book inspired by Francis of Assisi who is a model for our pope will help many to rediscover the gospel message for today.
—Jean Vanier, founder of L'Arche International

Since his election in March 2013, many, many people have been inspired by Pope Francis's profound spirituality and ability to articulate the deep love that God has for all people. Editor Alicia von Stamwitz has done a superb job in arranging the messages of Pope Francis in a manner that makes this book easy to use as a resource for prayer and reflection. This book will be treasured in the years to come as a remembrance of the first year of Pope Francis's papacy and the transformation his deep understanding of the Gospel is bringing to the people of God.
—Ron Rolheiser, O.M.I., author, speaker, and president of the Oblate School of Theology

Pope Francis is always so quotable that the challenge in a collection such as this is making smart choices. Fortunately, Alicia von Stamwitz is a (nearly) infallible guide!

—John L. Allen Jr., associate editor, *Crux* and *Boston Globe*

This is neither a pretentious book, nor a haughty one. Instead, it is a rich, quiet, assured book whose pages speak to, and about, the cumulative hope of the two millennia since Christ was here among us. As a body of selected writings and excerpts, it is both more deeply consoling and more religiously invigorating than I can even begin to say (and this from a life-long Protestant, no less) but this much I do know and can say: the Church Universal has arrived at a new and holier time. Thanks be to God.

—Phyllis Tickle, compiler, *The Divine Hours*

In his commitment to the poor, to peace, and to creation care Pope Francis is changing the status quo; challenging institutions of wealth and power, while inspiring the vulnerable and faithful around the world. The way Francis lives his life reminds us of Christ, and his message is reaching people of all religions and none. In *The Spirit of Saint Francis: Inspiring Words from Pope Francis,* Alicia von Stamwitz has compiled the pope's most powerful and uplifting words on a wide variety of critical topics for the health and future of God's children. I recommend this book to anyone looking for inspiration, vision, and spiritual guidance. These words of Pope Francis demonstrate why he is becoming such a life-changing, church-changing, and world changing leader—and a delightfully surprising gift from God.

—Jim Wallis, *New York Times* bestselling author of *The UnCommon Good* and president of Sojourners

Young people watch us: Do our actions match our words? In Pope Francis they—and we—find a person whose words about Jesus are illustrated by his actions on behalf of the young, the marginalized, the poor, and the oppressed. Pope Francis provides both insight and application on love, mercy, forgiveness, humility, joy, compassion. His words have power because his life is a powerful example of discipleship. He challenged the young Church at World Youth Day 2013 to go make a mess in the streets…and I would add, take this book along with you! It serves as a wonderful guide to encountering Jesus.

— Bob McCarty, executive director, National Federation for Catholic Youth Ministry

What a wonderful collection of reflections by Pope Francis! In such a short period of time, this relatively unknown shepherd who came from the ends of the earth has found a home in the minds and hearts of millions of people of good will around the world. He has managed to transmit to us the joy of the Gospel through simple words and profound gestures that have moved us deeply. Each Angelus address, daily homily, General Audience catechesis and major talk of Pope Francis contains gems of spirituality, pearls of Catholic doctrine and messages of hope for everyone. This little book offers a window onto Francis's Petrine Ministry and a doorway into his heart and mind.

—Fr. Thomas Rosica, C.S.B., CEO, Salt and Light Catholic Media Foundation, English Language Assistant to the Holy See Press Office

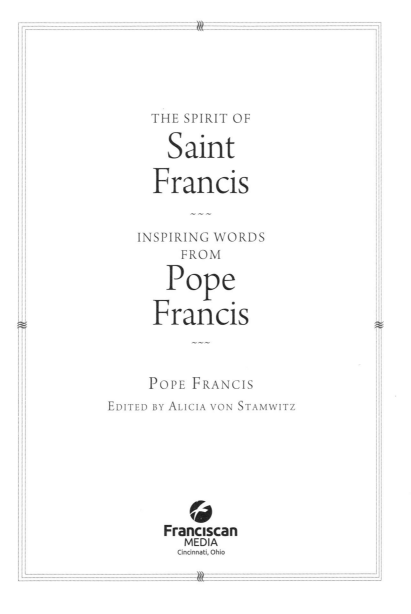

THE SPIRIT OF

Saint Francis

~~~

INSPIRING WORDS
FROM

Pope Francis

~~~

POPE FRANCIS

EDITED BY ALICIA VON STAMWITZ

Franciscan
MEDIA
Cincinnati, Ohio

The Spirit of St. Francis is published in collaboration with the Libreria Editrice Vaticana. All excerpts © 2015 Libreria Editrice Vaticana and used by permission. All rights reserved. Excerpts from Marion A. Habig, *St. Francis of Assisi: Writings and Early Biographies: English Omnibus of the Sources for the Life of St. Francis* (Cincinnati: Franciscan Media, 2012), are used by permission. All rights reserved. Excerpts from *The Francis Trilogy of Thomas of Celano: The Life of Saint Francis The Remembrance of the Desire of a Soul The Treatise on the Miracles of Saint Francis* by Regis J., Armstrong, O.F.M. Cap., J.A. Wayne Hellman, O.F.M. Conv., and William J. Short, O.F.M., eds. (Hyde Park: New City, 2004), are used by permission. All rights reserved.

Cover and book design by Mark Sullivan
Cover image © Giampiero Sposito | Reuters

LIBRARY OF CONGRESS CATALOGING-IN-PUBLICATION DATA
Francis, Pope, 1936-
  The spirit of Saint Francis : inspiring words from Pope Francis / Pope Francis ; edited by Alicia von Stamwitz.
      pages cm
  ISBN 978-1-61636-859-3 (alk. paper)
  1. Spiritual life—Catholic Church. 2. Christian life—Catholic authors. 3. Francis, of Assisi, Saint, 1182-1226. I. Stamwitz, Alicia von, editor. II. Title.
  BX2350.3.F748 2015
  230'.2—dc23
                                        2014038011

ISBN 978-1-61636-859-3

Copyright ©2015, Franciscan Media. All rights reserved.

Published by Franciscan Media
28 W. Liberty St.
Cincinnati, OH 45202
www.FranciscanMedia.org

Printed in the United States of America.
Printed on acid-free paper.
15 16 17 18 19 5 4 3 2 1

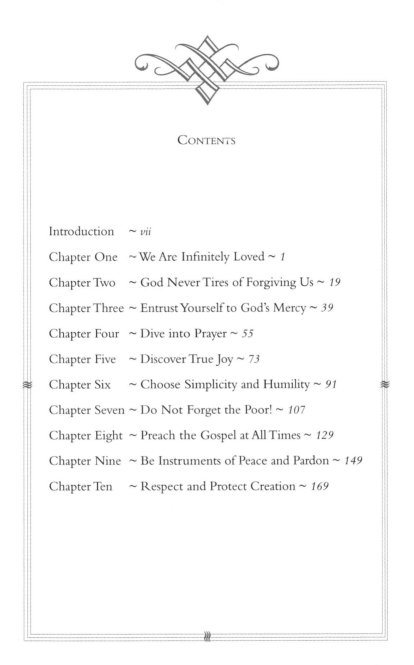

CONTENTS

Introduction

Some people want to know why I wished to be
called Francis. For me, Francis of Assisi is the man
of poverty, the man of peace, the man who loves
and protects creation.

—POPE FRANCIS, MARCH 16, 2013

By taking the name of one of the most venerated figures
in Christendom, Pope Francis set a high bar for his papacy.
The legacy of Francis of Assisi (1182–1226) is epic, a
breathtaking testament to divine love and the human
capacity for compassion, joy, and peace. God opened
Francis's eyes to the reality of the spiritual world, and in
response Francis divested himself of every personal and
social encumbrance. Rejoicing in hope, burning with
love, Francis set out to proclaim the Gospel of Jesus
Christ. His words, together with the witness of his life,
sparked thousands of conversions, long-overdue reforms
in the Church, and a spiritual movement that continues
to this day.

Since his election in March 2013, the pope's Franciscan
"accent" has become increasingly evident. His optimism,

creativity, courage, and playful sense of humor are reminiscent of the beloved saint. He too engages listeners with warmth and wit, embodying an irresistible, modern spirituality. The chapters of this book outline a manner of living that is at once faithful to the teachings of Jesus and illuminated by the spirit of "the poor little man" from Assisi. Moreover, they reveal the genius of a global leader whose message transcends religious boundaries. What, exactly, is Pope Francis's message? In a sentence, his message is: "God is love" (1 John 4:8). Love is the energy at the heart of the universe. Love created the world, love sustains the world, and love unites the world. In God's great heart, the heart that beats at the center of the universe, we are all connected, we are all one. More personally, the hope that Pope Francis articulates every day is that you will encounter the tender and transforming love of Jesus Christ.

A word about the genesis and development of this book. The quotations presented in these pages have been selected and arranged with care. They are taken directly from the official Vatican texts of Pope Francis's homilies, speeches, tweets, audiences, prayers, daily meditations, and writings. Fr. Guiseppe Costa, S.D.B, director of the Vatican Publishing House, has reviewed the text. This is notable because Pope Francis's words have sometimes been mistranslated or misrepresented. Be assured that the quotations in this book are accurate and are never taken out of context.

Finally, although the chapters and quotations have been arranged in a certain way, they may be read in any order. Let your experience and curiosity be your guide. Trust it, trust yourself, and trust that the message you most need to hear will find you. Whether you are at the beginning, middle, or end of your spiritual journey, may Pope Francis's words strengthen you and give you hope for the future. And may St. Francis of Assisi bless you as he blessed his companion Brother Leo nearly eight hundred years ago:

> The Lord bless you and keep you.
> May he show his face to you and have mercy.
> May he turn his countenance to you and give
> you peace.
> The Lord bless you!
>
> —BLESSING OF ST. FRANCIS OF ASSISI TO
> BROTHER LEO

—Alicia von Stamwitz,
editor

CHAPTER ONE

~ We Are Infinitely Loved ~

Among other words used in ordinary conversation, [Francis of Assisi] could never hear "the love of God" without a kind of transformation within himself.

For immediately upon hearing "the love of God," he would become excited, stirred, and inflamed, as though an inner chord of his heart had been plucked by the plectrum of the outward voice of the speaker....

"The love of him," he said, "who loved us much is much to be loved."[1]

—THOMAS OF CELANO,
The Second Life of Saint Francis

---

1. Celano quote from Marion A. Habig, *St. Francis of Assisi: Writings and Early Biographies: English Omnibus of the Sources for the Life of St. Francis* Cincinnati: Franciscan Media, 2012), pp. 519–520. Hereinafter called *Omnibus.* A plectrum is a tiny piece of ivory or metal, used in playing a lyre or other such stringed instrument.

God Is Waiting For You

The love of God precedes everything. God is always first. He arrives before us, he precedes us. The Prophet Isaiah, or Jeremiah, I don't remember, said that God is like an almond blossom, because it is the first tree to flower in spring, meaning that God always flowers before us. When we arrive he is waiting for us, he calls us, he makes us walk. Always anticipating us. And this is called love, because God always waits for us.

"But, Father, I don't believe this, because if you only knew, Father; my life was so horrible, how can I think that God is waiting for me?"

God is waiting for you. And if you were a great sinner, he is waiting for you even more and waiting for you with great love, because he is first. This is the beauty of the Church, who leads us to this God who is waiting for us! He precedes Abraham, he precedes even Adam.

GENERAL AUDIENCE, ST. PETER'S SQUARE
WEDNESDAY, JUNE 18, 2014

TRUST IN GOD'S LOVE

God is love. And we move towards the light to find the love of God. But is God's love within us, even in the dark moments? Is the love of God there, hidden away? Yes, always! The love of God never leaves us. It is always with us. Do we trust in this love?

ADDRESS TO CHILDREN, PAUL VI AUDIENCE HALL
SATURDAY, MAY 31, 2014

Pope Francis @Pontifex • November 11, 2013

"God loves us. May we discover the beauty of loving and being loved."

THE LORD CALLS YOU

I would like to say to those who feel far from God and from the Church—I would like to say respectfully—to all those who are fearful or indifferent: the Lord calls you too, he calls you to be a part of his people, and he does so with deep respect and love! The Lord is calling you. The Lord is seeking you. The Lord is waiting for you. The Lord does not proselytize, he loves, and this love seeks you, waits for you, you who at this moment do not believe this or are far away. And this is the love of God.

ANGELUS, ST. PETER'S SQUARE
MONDAY, JANUARY 6, 2014

God's Love Has a Name and a Face

What is God's love? It is not something vague, some generic feeling. God's love has a name and a face: Jesus Christ, Jesus. Love for God is made manifest in Jesus. For we cannot love air.... Do we love air? Do we love all things? No, no we cannot; we love people and the person we love is Jesus, the gift of the Father among us. It is a love that gives value and beauty to everything else; a love that gives strength to the family, to work, to study, to friendship, to art, to all human activity. It even gives meaning to negative experiences, because this love allows us to move beyond these experiences, to go beyond them, not to remain prisoners of evil. It moves us beyond, always opening us to hope, that's it! Love of God in Jesus always opens us to hope, to that horizon of hope, to the final horizon of our pilgrimage. In this way our labors and failures find meaning. Even our sin finds meaning in the love of God because this love of God in Jesus Christ always forgives us. He loves us so much that he always forgives us.

ANGELUS, ST. PETER'S SQUARE
SUNDAY, AUGUST 11, 2013

The Lord Chose You

"The Lord set his love upon you and chose you" (Dt 7:7).
God is bound to us, he chose us, and this bond is for ever,
not so much because we are faithful, but because the Lord
is faithful and endures our faithlessness, our indolence, our
lapses…. We can experience and savor the tenderness of
this love at every stage of life: in times of joy and of sadness,
in times of good health and of frailty and of sickness.

HOMILY, GEMELLI HOSPITAL AND
SACRED HEART UNIVERSITY
FRIDAY, JUNE 27, 2014

Pope Francis @Pontifex • March 22, 2014
"Jesus is our hope. Nothing—not even evil or death—is able
to separate us from the saving power of his love."

What is the Measure of God's Love?

The charity of Christ, welcomed with an open heart, changes us, transforms us, renders us capable of loving not according to human measure, always limited, but according to the measure of God. And what is the measure of God? Without measure! The measure of God is without measure. Everything! Everything! Everything! It's impossible to measure the love of God: it is without measure! And so we become capable of loving even those who do not love us: and this is not easy. To love someone who doesn't love us…. It's not easy! Because if we know that a person doesn't like us, then we also tend to bear ill will. But no! We must love even someone who doesn't love us! Opposing evil with good, with pardon, with sharing, with welcome.

ANGELUS, ST. PETER'S SQUARE
SUNDAY, JUNE 22, 2014

Our God is Real

The light of Eastertide and of Pentecost renews in us every year the joy and amazement of faith: let us recognize that God is not something vague, our God is not a God "spray," he is tangible; he is not abstract but has a name: "God is love." His is not a sentimental, emotional kind of love but the love of the Father who is the origin of all life, the love of the Son who dies on the Cross and is raised, the love of the Spirit who renews human beings and the world. Thinking that God is love does us so much good, because it teaches us to love, to give ourselves to others as Jesus gave himself to us and walks with us. Jesus walks beside us on the road through life.

ANGELUS, ST. PETER'S SQUARE
SUNDAY, MAY 26, 2013

The Stupendous Mystery of God's Love

Awareness of the marvels that the Lord has wrought for our salvation disposes our minds and hearts to an attitude of thanksgiving to God for all that he has given us, for all that he has accomplished for the good of his people and for the whole of humanity. This marks the beginning of our conversion: it is the grateful response to the stupendous mystery of God's love. When we see the love that God has for us, we feel the desire to draw close to him: this is conversion.

GENERAL AUDIENCE, ST. PETER'S SQUARE
ASH WEDNESDAY, MARCH 5, 2014

Pope Francis @Pontifex • February 7, 2014

"What zest life acquires when we allow ourselves to be filled by the love of God!"

TO LOVE AND BE LOVED

The heart of the human being aspires to great things, lofty values, deep friendships, ties that are strengthened rather than broken by the trials of life. The human being aspires to love and to be loved. This is our deepest aspiration: to love and be loved; and definitively. The culture of the temporary does not honor our freedom, but deprives us of our true destiny, of our truest and most authentic goals. It is a piecemeal life. It is sad to reach a certain age, to look back over the journey we have made and find that it was made up of different pieces, without unity, without decisiveness: everything temporary…. Do not allow yourselves to be robbed of the will to build great and lasting things in your life! This is what leads you forward. Do not content yourselves with little goals. Aspire to happiness, have courage, the courage to go outside of yourselves and bet on the fullness of your future together with Jesus.

ADDRESS TO THE YOUNG PEOPLE OF ABRUZZI
AND MOLISE, CASTELPETROSO CHURCH SQUARE
SATURDAY, JULY 5, 2014

GOD IS LIKE A MOTHER WITH HER BABY

As when a mother takes her child upon her knee and caresses him or her: so the Lord will do and does with us. This is the cascade of tenderness which gives us much consolation. "As one whom his mother comforts, so I will comfort you" (Is 66:13). Every Christian, and especially you and I, is called to be a bearer of this message of hope that gives serenity and joy: God's consolation, his tenderness towards all. But if we first experience the joy of being consoled by him, of being loved by him, then we can bring that joy to others. This is important if our mission is to be fruitful: to feel God's consolation and to pass it on to others!... Do not be afraid, because the Lord is the Lord of consolation, he is the Lord of tenderness. The Lord is a Father and he says that he will be for us like a mother with her baby, with a mother's tenderness.

HOMILY, ST. PETER'S BASILICA
SUNDAY, JULY 7, 2013

LOVE ALWAYS KINDLES NEW LOVE

The love of Jesus Christ lasts forever, it has no end because it is the very life of God. This love conquers sin and gives the strength to rise and begin again, for through forgiveness the heart is renewed and rejuvenated. We all know it: our Father never tires of loving and his eyes never grow weary of watching the road to his home to see if the son who left and was lost is returning. We can speak of God's hope: our Father expects us always, he doesn't just leave the door open to us, but he awaits us. He is engaged in the waiting for his children. And this Father also does not tire of loving the other son who, though staying at home with him the whole time, does not share in his mercy, in his compassion. God is not only at the origin of love, but in Jesus Christ he calls us to imitate his own way of loving: "As I have loved you, may you also love one another" (Jn 13:34). To the extent to which Christians live this love, they become credible disciples of Christ to the world. Love cannot bear being locked up in itself. By its nature it is open, it spreads and bears fruit, it always kindles new love.

HOMILY, ST. PETER'S BASILICA
FRIDAY, MARCH 28, 2014

Pope Francis @Pontifex • May 30, 2013

"The whole of salvation history is the story of God looking for us: he offers us love and welcomes us with tenderness."

CARRY THE GOSPEL EVERYWHERE

Dear families, dear brothers and sisters, I encourage you to carry the Gospel of Jesus Christ everywhere, even to those most de-Christianized, especially in the margins of life. Evangelize with love, bring God's love to all. Tell all those you meet on the streets of your mission that God loves man as he is, even with his limitations, with his mistakes, even with his sins. That is why he sent his Son, that he might take our sins onto himself. May you be messengers and witnesses of the infinite goodness and inexhaustible mercy of the Father.

ADDRESS TO REPRESENTATIVES OF THE
NEOCATECHUMENAL WAY, PAUL VI AUDIENCE HALL
SATURDAY, FEBRUARY 1, 2014

MAKE KNOWN OUR BELOVED GOD

The primary reason for evangelizing is the love of Jesus which we have received, the experience of salvation which urges us to ever greater love of him. What kind of love would not feel the need to speak of the beloved, to point him out, to make him known? If we do not feel an intense desire to share this love, we need to pray insistently that he will once more touch our hearts. We need to implore his grace daily, asking him to open our cold hearts and shake up our lukewarm and superficial existence. Standing before him with open hearts, letting him look at us, we see that gaze of love which Nathaniel glimpsed on the day when Jesus said to him: "I saw you under the fig tree" (Jn 1:48).

APOSTOLIC EXHORTATION, *EVANGELII GAUDIUM*, 264
NOVEMBER 24, 2013

PROCLAIM THE MESSAGE: "GOD IS LOVE!"

We are all called to witness and proclaim the message that "God is love," that God isn't far and insensitive to our human affairs. He is close to us, always beside us, walking with us to share our joys and our sorrows, our hopes and our struggles. He loves us very much and for that reason he became man, he came into the world not to condemn it, but so the world would be saved through Jesus (cf. Jn 3:16–17). And this is the love of God in Jesus, this love that is so difficult to understand but that we feel when we draw close to Jesus. And he always forgives us, he always awaits us, he loves us so much. And we feel the love of Jesus and the love of God.

ANGELUS, ST. PETER'S SQUARE
SUNDAY, JUNE 15, 2014

GOD MAKES ALL THINGS NEW

You see, the new things of God are not like the novelties of this world, all of which are temporary; they come and go, and we keep looking for more. The new things which God gives to our lives are lasting, not only in the future, when we will be with him, but today as well. God is even now making all things new; the Holy Spirit is truly transforming us, and through us he also wants to transform the world in which we live. Let us open the doors to the Spirit, let ourselves be guided by him, and allow God's constant help to make us new men and women, inspired by the love of God which the Holy Spirit bestows on us! How beautiful it would be if each of you, every evening, could say: Today at school, at home, at work, guided by God, I showed a sign of love towards one of my friends, my parents, an older person! How beautiful!

HOMILY, ST. PETER'S SQUARE
SUNDAY, APRIL 28, 2013

One Heart, One Soul

John's Gospel states that, before his Passion, Jesus prayed to the Father for communion among his disciples with these words: "That they may all be one; even as thou, Father, art in me, and I in thee, that they also may be in us, so that the world may believe that thou hast sent me" (17:21). The Church, in her most profound truth, is communion with God, intimacy with God, a communion of love with Christ and with the Father in the Holy Spirit, which extends to brotherly communion. This relationship between Jesus and the Father is the "matrix" of the bond between us Christians: if we are intimately part of this "matrix," this fiery furnace of love, then we can truly become of one single heart and one single soul among us. For God's love burns away our selfishness, our prejudices, our interior and exterior divisions. The love of God even burns away our sins.

GENERAL AUDIENCE, ST. PETER'S SQUARE
WEDNESDAY, OCTOBER 30, 2013

No Act of Love for God Will Be Lost

We may be sure that none of our acts of love will be lost, nor any of our acts of sincere concern for others. No single act of love for God will be lost, no generous effort is meaningless, no painful endurance is wasted. All of these encircle our world like a vital force. Sometimes it seems that our work is fruitless, but mission is not like a business transaction or investment, or even a humanitarian activity. It is not a show where we count how many people come as a result of our publicity; it is something much deeper, which escapes all measurement. It may be that the Lord uses our sacrifices to shower blessings in another part of the world which we will never visit. The Holy Spirit works as he wills, when he wills and where he wills; we entrust ourselves without pretending to see striking results. We know only that our commitment is necessary. Let us learn to rest in the tenderness of the arms of the Father amid our creative and generous commitment. Let us keep marching forward; let us give him everything, allowing him to make our efforts bear fruit in his good time.

APOSTOLIC EXHORTATION, *EVANGELII GAUDIUM*, 279
NOVEMBER 24, 2013

CHAPTER TWO

~ God Never Tires of Forgiving Us ~

One day [Francis of Assisi] was marveling at the Lord's mercy in the kindness shown to him. He wished that the Lord would show him the course of life for him and his brothers, and he went to a place of prayer, as he so often did. He remained there a long time with fear and trembling before the Ruler of the whole earth. He recalled in the bitterness of his soul the years he spent badly, frequently repeating this phrase: "Lord, be merciful to me, a sinner." Gradually, an indescribable joy and tremendous sweetness began to well up deep in his heart.[2]

—THOMAS OF CELANO,
The First Life of St. Francis

2. Regis J. Armstrong, O.F.M. Cap., J.A. Wayne Hellman, O.F.M. Conv., and William J. Short, O.F.M., eds., *The Francis Trilogy of Thomas of Celano: The Life of Saint Francis; The Remembrance of the Desire of a Soul; The Treatise on the Miracles of Saint Francis* (New York: New City, 2004), p. 45. Hereinafter called *Trilogy*.

TEACH US, ST. FRANCIS, TO ACCEPT GOD'S FORGIVENESS
What does Saint Francis' witness tell us today? What does he have to say to us, not merely with words—that is easy enough—but by his life?...

The first thing he tells us is this: that being a Christian means having a living relationship with the person of Jesus; it means putting on Christ, being conformed to him.

Where did Francis's journey to Christ begin? It began with the gaze of the crucified Jesus. With letting Jesus look at us at the very moment that he gives his life for us and draws us to himself. Francis experienced this in a special way in the Church of San Damiano, as he prayed before the cross which I too will have an opportunity to venerate....

The cross does not speak to us about defeat and failure; paradoxically, it speaks to us about a death which is life, a death which gives life, for it speaks to us of love, the love of God incarnate, a love which does not die, but triumphs over evil and death. When we let the crucified Jesus gaze upon us, we are re-created, we become "a new creation." Everything else starts with this: the experience of transforming grace, the experience of being loved for no merits of our own, in spite of our being sinners. That is why St. Francis could say with St. Paul: "Far be it from me to glory except in the cross of our Lord Jesus Christ" (Gal 6:14).

We turn to you, Francis, and we ask you: Teach us to remain before the cross, to let the crucified Christ gaze upon us, to let ourselves be forgiven, and to be recreated by his love.

HOMILY, ST. FRANCIS SQUARE, ASSISI
FRIDAY, OCTOBER 4, 2013

GOD'S PLAN OF LOVE AND SALVATION

God created us so that we might live in a profound
relationship of friendship with him, and even when sin
broke off this relationship with him, with others and with
creation, God did not abandon us. The entire history
of salvation is the story of God who seeks out human
beings, offers them his love and welcomes them. He called
Abraham to be the father of a multitude, he chose the
people of Israel to make a covenant that would embrace
all peoples, and in the fullness of time, he sent forth his Son
so that his plan of love and salvation might be fulfilled in
a new and eternal covenant with the whole of humanity.

GENERAL AUDIENCE, ST. PETER'S SQUARE
WEDNESDAY, MAY 29, 2013

Jesus Takes Away the Sin of the World

Jesus is called the Lamb: He is the Lamb who takes away the sin of the world. Someone might think: but how can a lamb, which is so weak, a weak little lamb, how can it take away so many sins, so much wickedness? With love. With his meekness. Jesus never ceased being a lamb: meek, good, full of love, close to the little ones, close to the poor. He was there, among the people, healing everyone, teaching, praying. Jesus, so weak, like a lamb. However, he had the strength to take all our sins upon himself, all of them. "But, Father, you don't know my life: I have a sin so heavy that I can't even carry it with a truck." Many times, when we examine our conscience, we find some sins there that are truly bad! But he carries them. He came for this: to forgive, to make peace in the world—but first to make peace in our hearts.

HOMILY, SACRED HEART OF JESUS PARISH
SUNDAY, JANUARY 19, 2014

THE WOUNDS OF JESUS

When Jesus returns to heaven, he brings the Father a gift. What is the gift? His wounds. His body is very beautiful, no bruises, no cuts from the scourging, but he retains his wounds. When he returns to the Father he shows him the wounds and says: "Behold, Father, this is the price of the pardon you have granted." When the Father beholds the wounds of Jesus he forgives us forever, not because we are good, but because Jesus paid for us. Beholding the wounds of Jesus, the Father becomes most merciful. This is the great work of Jesus today in heaven: showing the Father the price of forgiveness, his wounds. This is the beauty that urges us not to be afraid to ask forgiveness. The Father always pardons, because he sees the wounds of Jesus, he sees our sin and he forgives it.

REGINA CAELI, ST. PETER'S SQUARE
SUNDAY, JUNE 1, 2014

There Is No Sin God Cannot Forgive

Let us not be closed to the newness that God wants to bring into our lives! Are we often weary, disheartened and sad? Do we feel weighed down by our sins? Do we think that we won't be able to cope? Let us not close our hearts, let us not lose confidence, let us never give up: there are no situations which God cannot change, there is no sin which he cannot forgive if only we open ourselves to him.

HOMILY, ST. PETER'S BASILICA
HOLY SATURDAY, MARCH 30, 2013

Pope Francis @Pontifex • March 4, 2014
"In life we all make many mistakes. Let us learn to recognize our errors and ask forgiveness."

THE SPIRIT OF ST. FRANCIS

THE LORD NEVER DISAPPOINTS

In listening to what John the Baptist says, who bears witness to Jesus as the Savior, our confidence in Jesus should grow. Many times we trust a doctor: this is good, because the doctor is there to cure us. We trust in a person: this too is good, because brothers and sisters can help us. It is good to have this human trust among ourselves. But we forget about trust in the Lord: this is the key to success in life. Trust in the Lord, let us trust in the Lord!...

Listen carefully, young people, who are just beginning life now: Jesus never disappoints. Never. This is the testimony of John: Jesus, the good One, the meek One, will end as a lamb, who is slain. Without crying out. He came to save us, to take away sin. Mine, yours and that of the whole world: all of it, all of it.

And now I invite you to do something: let us close our eyes, let us imagine the scene on the banks of the river, John as he is baptizing and Jesus who is approaching. And let us listen to John's voice: "Behold, the Lamb of God, who takes away the sin of the world." Let us watch Jesus and, in silence, each one of us, say something to Jesus from his or her heart. In silence.

HOMILY, SACRED HEART OF JESUS PARISH
SUNDAY, JANUARY 19, 2014

Pope Francis @Pontifex • December 2, 2013

"Your sins are great? Just tell the Lord: Forgive me, help me to get up again, change my heart!"

WE ARE IN SAFE HANDS

In Christ, true God and true man, our humanity was taken to God. Christ opened the path to us. He is like a roped guide climbing a mountain who, on reaching the summit, pulls us up to him and leads us to God. If we entrust our life to him, if we let ourselves be guided by him, we are certain to be in safe hands, in the hands of our Savior, of our Advocate.

GENERAL AUDIENCE, ST. PETER'S SQUARE
WEDNESDAY, APRIL 17, 2013

COME OUT, I GIVE YOU LIFE!

We all have within us some areas, some parts of our heart, that are not alive, that are a little dead; and some of us have many dead places in our hearts, a true spiritual necrosis! And when we are in this situation, we know it, we want to get out but we can't. Only the power of Jesus, the power of Jesus, can help us come out of these atrophied zones of the heart, these tombs of sin, which we all have. We are all sinners! But if we become very attached to these tombs and guard them within us and do not will that our whole heart rise again to life, we become corrupted and our soul begins to give off, as Martha says, an "odor" (Jn 11:39), the stench of a person who is attached to sin. And Lent is a bit for this: so that all of us, who are sinners, do not end up attached to sin but can hear what Jesus said to Lazarus: "He cried out with a loud voice: 'Lazarus, come out'" (Jn 11:43).

Today I invite you to think for a moment, in silence, here: where is my interior necrosis? Where is the dead part of my soul? Where is my tomb? Think, for a short moment, all of you in silence. Let us think: what part of the heart can be corrupted because of my attachment to sin, one sin or another? And to remove the stone, to take away the stone of shame and allow the Lord to say to us, as he said to Lazarus: "Come out!" so that all our soul might be healed, might be raised by the love of Jesus, by the power of Jesus. He is capable of forgiving us. We all need it! All of us. We are all sinners, but we must be careful not to become corrupt! Sinners we may be, but He forgives us. Let us hear that voice of Jesus who, by the power of God, says to us: "Come out! Leave that tomb you have within you. Come out. I give you life, I give you happiness, I bless you, I want you for myself."

HOMILY, SAN GREGORIO MAGNO CHURCH
SUNDAY, APRIL 6, 2014

THE CROSS IS MORE THAN AN ORNAMENT

The heart of God's salvation is his Son who took upon himself our sins, our pride, our self reliance, our vanity, our desire to be like God. A Christian who is not able to glory in Christ Crucified has not understood what it means to be Christian. Our wounds, those which sin leaves in us, are healed only through the Lord's wounds, through the wounds of God-made-man who humbled himself, who emptied himself. This is the mystery of the Cross. It is not only an ornament that we always put in churches, on the altar; it is not only a symbol that should distinguish us from others. The Cross is a mystery: the mystery of the love of God who humbles himself, who empties himself to save us from our sins.

MORNING MEDITATION, ST. MARTHA'S HOUSE
TUESDAY, APRIL 8, 2014

Jesus Christ Loves You

On the lips of the catechist the first proclamation must ring out over and over: "Jesus Christ loves you; he gave his life to save you; and now he is living at your side every day to enlighten, strengthen and free you."

APOSTOLIC EXHORTATION, *EVANGELII GAUDIUM,* 164
NOVEMBER 24, 2013

The Peace that Only Jesus Can Give

Forgiveness is not the fruit of our own efforts but rather a gift, it is a gift of the Holy Spirit who fills us with the wellspring of mercy and of grace that flows unceasingly from the open heart of the crucified and risen Christ. Secondly, it reminds us that we can truly be at peace only if we allow ourselves to be reconciled, in the Lord Jesus, with the Father and with the brethren. And we have all felt this in our hearts, when we have gone to confession with a soul weighed down and with a little sadness; but then when we receive Jesus' forgiveness and we feel at peace, with that peace of soul which is so beautiful, and which only Jesus can give, only him.

GENERAL AUDIENCE, ST. PETER'S SQUARE
WEDNESDAY, FEBRUARY 19, 2014

THE RE-CREATION OF THE WORLD

Reconciliation is the re-creation of the world; and the most profound mission of Jesus is the redemption of all of us sinners. And Jesus did not do this with words, with actions or by walking on the road: no! He did it with his flesh. It is truly he, God, who becomes one of us, a man, to heal us from within.

MORNING MEDITATION, ST. MARTHA'S HOUSE
THURSDAY, JULY 4, 2013

GOD ACCOMPANIES US

God, when he forgives us, he accompanies us and helps us along the way. Always. Even in the small things. When we go to confession, the Lord tells us: "I forgive you. But now come with me." And he helps us to get back on the path. He never condemns. He never simply forgives, but he forgives and accompanies. Then we are fragile and we have to return to confession, everyone. But he never tires. He always takes us by the hand again. This is the love of God, and we must imitate it! Society must imitate it. Take this path.

ADDRESS AT THE PENITENTIARY IN CASTROVILLARI
SATURDAY, JUNE 21, 2014

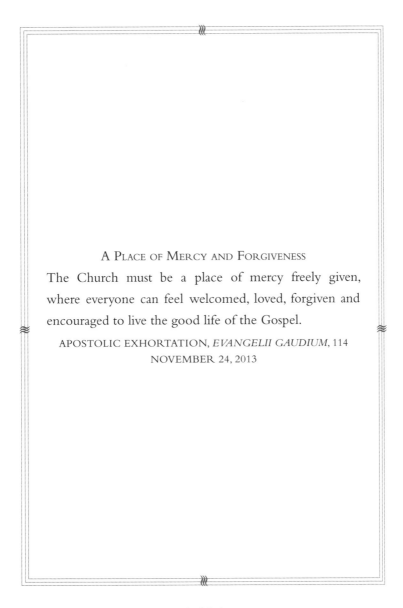

A PLACE OF MERCY AND FORGIVENESS

The Church must be a place of mercy freely given, where everyone can feel welcomed, loved, forgiven and encouraged to live the good life of the Gospel.

APOSTOLIC EXHORTATION, *EVANGELII GAUDIUM*, 114
NOVEMBER 24, 2013

With God We Can Do Great Things

Remain steadfast in the journey of faith, with firm hope in the Lord. This is the secret of our journey! He gives us the courage to swim against the tide. Pay attention, my young friends: to go against the current; this is good for the heart, but we need courage to swim against the tide. Jesus gives us this courage! There are no difficulties, trials or misunderstandings to fear, provided we remain united to God as branches to the vine, provided we do not lose our friendship with him, provided we make ever more room for him in our lives. This is especially so whenever we feel poor, weak and sinful, because God grants strength to our weakness, riches to our poverty, conversion and forgiveness to our sinfulness. The Lord is so rich in mercy: every time, if we go to him, he forgives us. Let us trust in God's work! With him we can do great things; he will give us the joy of being his disciples, his witnesses. Commit yourselves to great ideals, to the most important things. We Christians were not chosen by the Lord for little things; push onwards toward the highest principles. Stake your lives on noble ideals, my dear young people!

HOMILY, CONFIRMATION MASS, ST. PETER'S SQUARE
SUNDAY, APRIL 28, 2013

Pope Francis @Pontifex • June 19, 2014

"There is never a reason to lose hope. Jesus says: 'I am with you until the end of the world.'"

NEVER FORGET GOD'S MERCY

The Church is the great family of God's children. Of course, she also has human aspects. In those who make up the Church, pastors and faithful, there are shortcomings, imperfections and sins. The Pope has these too—and many of them; but what is beautiful is that when we realize we are sinners we encounter the mercy of God who always forgives. Never forget it: God always pardons us and receives us into his love and mercy. Some people say that sin is an offence to God, but also an opportunity to humble oneself so as to realize that there is something else more beautiful: God's mercy. Let us think about this.

GENERAL AUDIENCE, ST. PETER'S SQUARE
WEDNESDAY, MAY 29, 2013

CHAPTER THREE

~ Entrust Yourself to God's Mercy ~

With all our hearts and all our souls,
all our minds and all our strength,
with every faculty and every effort,
with every affection and all our emotions,
with every wish and desire,
we should love our Lord and God
who has given and gives us everything,
body and soul, and all our life;
it was he who created and redeemed us
and of his mercy alone he will save us…
He has provided us with every good
and does not cease to provide for us.[3]

—ST. FRANCIS OF ASSISI,
The Earlier Rule

3. *Omnibus,* pp. 51–52.

The Immensity of God's Mercy

God placed on Jesus' cross all the weight of our sins, all the injustices perpetrated by every Cain against his brother, all the bitterness of the betrayal by Judas and by Peter, all the vanity of tyrants, all the arrogance of false friends. It was a heavy cross, like night experienced by abandoned people, heavy like the death of loved ones, heavy because it carries all the ugliness of evil. However, the cross is also glorious like the dawn after a long night, for it represents all the love of God, which is greater than our iniquities and our betrayals. In the cross we see the monstrosity of man, when he allows evil to guide him; but we also see the immensity of the mercy of God, who does not treat us according to our sins but according to his mercy.

WAY OF THE CROSS, PALATINE HILL
GOOD FRIDAY, APRIL 18, 2014

Pope Francis @Pontifex • March 24, 2014
"Jesus is never far from us sinners. He wants to pour out on us, without limit, all of his mercy."

OPEN YOUR HEART TO GOD'S GOODNESS AND MERCY

We frequently fail to grasp the plan of God, and we realize that we are not capable of assuring ourselves of happiness and eternal life. It is precisely in experiencing our own limitations and our poverty, however, that the Holy Spirit comforts us and lets us perceive that the only important thing is to allow ourselves to be led by Jesus into the Father's arms.

This is why we need this gift of the Holy Spirit so much. Fear of the Lord allows us to be aware that everything comes from grace and that our true strength lies solely in following the Lord Jesus and in allowing the Father to bestow upon us his goodness and his mercy. To open the heart, so that the goodness and mercy of God may come to us. This is what the Holy Spirit does through the gift of fear of the Lord: he opens hearts. The heart opens so that forgiveness, mercy, goodness and the caress of the Father may come to us, for as children we are infinitely loved.

GENERAL AUDIENCE, ST. PETER'S SQUARE
WEDNESDAY, JUNE 11, 2014

Enveloped by Mercy

In my own life, I have so often seen God's merciful countenance, his patience; I have also seen so many people find the courage to enter the wounds of Jesus by saying to him: Lord, I am here, accept my poverty, hide my sin in your wounds, wash it away with your blood. And I have always seen that God did just this—he accepted them, consoled them, cleansed them, loved them.

Dear brothers and sisters, let us be enveloped by the mercy of God; let us trust in his patience, which always gives us more time. Let us find the courage to return to his house, to dwell in his loving wounds, allowing ourselves be loved by him and to encounter his mercy in the sacraments. We will feel his wonderful tenderness, we will feel his embrace, and we too will become more capable of mercy, patience, forgiveness and love.

HOMILY, BASILICA OF SAINT JOHN LATERAN
DIVINE MERCY SUNDAY, APRIL 7, 2013

God Draws Us to Himself

The salvation which God offers us is the work of his mercy. No human efforts, however good they may be, can enable us to merit so great a gift. God, by his sheer grace, draws us to himself and makes us one with him. He sends his Spirit into our hearts to make us his children, transforming us and enabling us to respond to his love by our lives.

APOSTOLIC EXHORTATION, *EVANGELII GAUDIUM*, 112
NOVEMBER 24, 2013

Pope Francis @Pontifex • April 7, 2013
"How beautiful is the gaze with which Jesus regards us—how full of tenderness! Let us never lose trust in the patience and mercy of God."

GO TO JESUS, HE EMBRACES YOU

It is not easy to entrust oneself to God's mercy, because it is an abyss beyond our comprehension. But we must!

"Oh, Father, if you knew my life, you would not say that to me!"

"Why, what have you done?"

"Oh, I am a great sinner!"

"All the better! Go to Jesus: he likes you to tell him these things!"

He forgets, he has a very special capacity for forgetting. He forgets, he kisses you, he embraces you and he simply says to you: "Neither do I condemn you; go, and sin no more" (Jn 8:11).

HOMILY, ST. ANNA CHURCH
SUNDAY, MARCH 17, 2013

GOD'S MERCY IS A LIFE-GIVING FORCE

The mercy of Jesus is not only an emotion; it is a force which gives life that raises man! Today's Gospel also tells us this in the episode of the widow of Nain (Lk 7:11–17). With his disciples, Jesus arrives in Nain, a village in Galilee, right at the moment when a funeral is taking place. A boy, the only son of a widow, is being carried for burial. Jesus immediately fixes his gaze on the crying mother. The Evangelist Luke says: "And when the Lord saw her, he had compassion on her."....What is the fruit of this love and mercy? It is life! Jesus says to the widow of Nain: "Do not weep," and then he calls the dead boy and awakes him as if from sleep. Let's think about this, it's beautiful: God's mercy gives life to man, it raises him from the dead. Let us not forget that the Lord always watches over us with mercy; he always watches over us with mercy. Let us not be afraid of approaching him! He has a merciful heart! If we show him our inner wounds, our inner sins, he will always forgive us. It is pure mercy. Let us go to Jesus!

ANGELUS, ST. PETER'S SQUARE
SUNDAY, JUNE 9, 2013

TRANSFORMED BY MERCY

From the earliest times the Church of Rome has honored the Apostles Peter and Paul in a single feast on the same day, the 29th of June. They both welcomed God's love and allowed themselves to be transformed by his mercy; they thus became friends and apostles of Christ. This is why they continue to speak to the Church and still today they show us the way to salvation. And should we perchance fall into the most serious sins and the darkest of nights, God is always capable of transforming us too, the way he transformed Peter and Paul; transforming the heart and forgiving us for everything, thus transforming the darkness of our sin into a dawn of light. God is like this: he transforms us, he always forgives us, as he did with Peter and as he did with Paul.

ANGELUS, ST. PETER'S SQUARE
SUNDAY, JUNE 29, 2014

THE LORD JESUS POURS HIS MERCY UPON US

Jesus' gesture at the Last Supper is the ultimate thanksgiving to the Father for his love, for his mercy. "Thanksgiving" in Greek is expressed as "eucharist." And that is why the sacrament is called the Eucharist: it is the supreme thanksgiving to the Father, who so loved us that he gave us his Son out of love. This is why the term Eucharist includes the whole of that act, which is the act of God and man together, the act of Jesus Christ, true God and true Man....The Eucharist is the summit of God's saving action: the Lord Jesus, by becoming bread broken for us, pours upon us all of his mercy and his love, so as to renew our hearts, our lives and our way of relating with him and with the brethren.

GENERAL AUDIENCE, ST. PETER'S SQUARE
WEDNESDAY, FEBRUARY 5, 2014

Pope Francis @Pontifex • May 6, 2013
Let us ask our Lord to help us bear shining witness to his mercy and his love in every area of our Christian lives.

Be Merciful, Just as Your Father is Merciful

The way we treat others has a transcendent dimension: "The measure you give will be the measure you get" (Mt 7:2). It corresponds to the mercy which God has shown us: "Be merciful, just as your Father is merciful. Do not judge, and you will not be judged; do not condemn, and you will not be condemned. Forgive, and you will be forgiven; give, and it will be given to you....For the measure you give will be the measure you get back" (Lk 6:36–38). What these passages make clear is the absolute priority of "going forth from ourselves towards our brothers and sisters" as one of the two great commandments which ground every moral norm and as the clearest sign for discerning spiritual growth in response to God's completely free gift.

APOSTOLIC EXHORTATION, *EVANGELII GAUDIUM*, 179
NOVEMBER 24, 2013

THE CONFESSIONAL MUST NOT BE A TORTURE CHAMBER
I want to remind priests that the confessional must not be a torture chamber but rather an encounter with the Lord's mercy which spurs us on to do our best. A small step, in the midst of great human limitations, can be more pleasing to God than a life which appears outwardly in order but moves through the day without confronting great difficulties. Everyone needs to be touched by the comfort and attraction of God's saving love, which is mysteriously at work in each person, above and beyond their faults and failings.

APOSTOLIC EXHORTATION, *EVANGELII GAUDIUM*, 44
NOVEMBER 24, 2013

Be An Architect of Mercy

Whoever experiences divine mercy is impelled to be an architect of mercy among the least and the poor. In these "littlest brothers" Jesus awaits us (cf. Mt 25:40); let us receive mercy and let us give mercy! Let us go to the encounter and let us celebrate Easter in the joy of God!

HOMILY, ST. PETER'S BASILICA
FRIDAY, MARCH 28, 2014

Pope Francis @Pontifex • October 7, 2013

"Mercy is the true power that can save humanity and the world from sin and evil."

Mercy Has Triumphed

The Church throughout the world echoes the angel's message to the women: "Do not be afraid! I know that you are looking for Jesus who was crucified. He is not here; for he has been raised.... Come, see the place where he lay" (Mt 28:5–6).

This is the culmination of the Gospel, it is the Good News par excellence: Jesus, who was crucified, is risen! This event is the basis of our faith and our hope. If Christ were not raised, Christianity would lose its very meaning; the whole mission of the Church would lose its impulse, for this is the point from which it first set out and continues to set out ever anew. The message which Christians bring to the world is this: Jesus, Love incarnate, died on the cross for our sins, but God the Father raised him and made him the Lord of life and death. In Jesus, love has triumphed over hatred, mercy over sinfulness, goodness over evil, truth over falsehood, life over death.

URBI ET ORBI, LOGGIA OF ST. PETER'S BASILICA
SUNDAY, APRIL 20, 2014

The True Face of God

Give glory to God, for he is good, he is faithful, he is merciful. Today I voice my hope that everyone will come to know the true face of God, the Father who has given us Jesus. My hope is that everyone will feel God's closeness, live in his presence, love him and adore him. May each of us give glory to God above all by our lives, by lives spent for love of him and of all our brothers and sisters.

URBI ET ORBI, LOGGIA OF ST. PETER'S BASILICA
WEDNESDAY, DECEMBER 25, 2013

THIS IS THE GREAT TIME OF MERCY!

The manifestation of the Son of God on earth marks the beginning of the great time of mercy, after sin had closed the heavens, raising itself as a barrier between the human being and his Creator. With the birth of Jesus the heavens open! God gives us in Christ the guarantee of an indestructible love. From the moment the Word became flesh it is therefore possible to see the open heavens. It was possible for the shepherds of Bethlehem, for the Magi of the East, for the Baptist, for Jesus' Apostles, and for St. Stephen, the first martyr, who exclaimed: "Behold, I see the heavens opened!" (Acts 7:56). And it is possible for each one of us if we allow ourselves to be suffused with God's love, which is given to us for the first time in baptism by means of the Holy Spirit. Let us allow ourselves to be invaded by God's love! This is the great time of mercy! Do not forget it: this is the great time of mercy!

ANGELUS, ST. PETER'S SQUARE
SUNDAY, JANUARY 12, 2014

CHAPTER FOUR

~ Dive into Prayer ~

Often, without moving his lips,
St. Francis would meditate for a long time and,
concentrating, centering his external powers,
he would rise in spirit to heaven.
Thus, he directed his whole mind and affections
to the one thing he was asking of God.
He was not then so much a man who prayed,
as a man who had become a living prayer.[4]

—Thomas of Celano,
The Second Life of Saint Francis

---

4. Murray Bodo, *The Simple Way: Meditations on the Words of Saint Francis* (Cincinnati: Franciscan Media, 2009), p. 104. See also *Omnibus*, p. 440.

THE SEA OF GOD'S BOUNDLESS LOVE

Prayer is the strength of the Christian and of every person who believes. In the weakness and frailty of our lives, we can turn to God with the confidence of children and enter into communion with him. In the face of so many wounds that hurt us and could harden our hearts, we are called to dive into the sea of prayer, which is the sea of God's boundless love, to taste his tenderness.

HOMILY, BASILICA OF SANTA SABINA
ASH WEDNESDAY, MARCH 5, 2014

Pope Francis @Pontifex • June 28, 2014

"To be friends with God means to pray with simplicity, like children talking to their parents."

A Relationship Lived with the Heart

This relationship with the Lord is not intended as a duty or an imposition. It is a bond that comes from within. It is a relationship lived with the heart: it is our friendship with God, granted to us by Jesus, a friendship that changes our life and fills us with passion, with joy. Thus, the gift of piety stirs in us above all gratitude and praise. This is, in fact, the reason and the most authentic meaning of our worship and our adoration. When the Holy Spirit allows us to perceive the presence of the Lord and all his love for us, it warms the heart and moves us quite naturally to prayer and celebration.

GENERAL AUDIENCE, ST. PETER'S SQUARE
WEDNESDAY, JUNE 4, 2014

THE DAY I FIRST HEARD JESUS' VOICE

I want to tell you of a personal experience. Yesterday I celebrated the 60th anniversary of the day when I heard Jesus' voice in my heart. I am telling you this not so that you will make me a cake here; no, that is not why I'm saying it. However, it is a commemoration: 60 years since that day. I will never forget it. The Lord made me strongly aware that I should take that path. I was 17 years old. Several years passed before I made this decision, before this invitation became concrete and definitive. So many years have gone by, with some successes and joys, but also many years with failures, frailties, sin…60 years on the Lord's road, behind him, beside him, always with him. I only tell you this: I have no regrets! I have no regrets! Why? Because I feel like Tarzan and I feel strong enough to go ahead? No, I have not regretted it because always, even at the darkest moments, the moments of sin and moments of frailty, moments of failure, I have looked at Jesus and trusted in him and he has not deserted me. Trust in Jesus: he always keeps on going, he goes with us! However, listen, he never let us down. He is faithful, he is a faithful companion.

ADDRESS TO YOUNG PEOPLE, CAGLIARI
SUNDAY, SEPTEMBER 22, 2013

May You Feel the Lord's Presence in Your Life

Dear young people, love Jesus Christ more and more! Our life is a response to his call and you will be happy and will build your life well if you can answer this call. May you feel the Lord's presence in your life. He is close to each one of you as a companion, as a friend who knows how to help and understand you, who encourages you in difficult times and never abandons you. In prayer, in conversation with him and in reading the Bible, you will discover that he is truly close. You will also learn to read God's signs in your life. He always speaks to us, also through the events of our time and our daily life; it is up to us to listen to him.

ADDRESS TO STUDENTS OF JESUIT SCHOOLS,
PAUL VI AUDIENCE HALL
FRIDAY, JUNE 7, 2013

Pope Francis @Pontifex • May 19, 2014

"The one who listens attentively to the Word of God and truly prays, always asks the Lord: what is your will for me?"

TAKE A STEP FORWARD IN LOVE

We all have our likes and dislikes, and perhaps at this very moment we are angry with someone. At least let us say to the Lord: "Lord, I am angry with this person, with that person. I pray to you for him and for her." To pray for a person with whom I am irritated is a beautiful step forward in love, and an act of evangelization. Let us do it today! Let us not allow ourselves to be robbed of the ideal of fraternal love!

APOSTOLIC EXHORTATION, *EVANGELII GAUDIUM*, 101
NOVEMBER 24, 2013

My Ideal Prayer Practice

In the morning I try to pray Lauds and spend a little time in prayer, in *lectio divina* with the Lord.... And then, I celebrate Mass. Then the work begins: one day it's one kind of work and another day it's something else.... I try to do one thing at a time. Lunch is at noon, then a little siesta. After the siesta, at three o'clock—excuse me—I say Vespers, at three.... If they aren't said then, they won't be said at all! There's also reading, the Office of Readings for the next day. Then afternoon work, the things I am obliged to do.... Then, I spend a little time in Adoration and pray the rosary; dinner, and then I'm done. That's how it goes....

But sometimes not everything gets done, because I let myself be led by imprudent demands: too much work, or thinking that if I don't do this today, I won't do it tomorrow.... Adoration falls by the wayside, my siesta falls by the wayside, this or that falls by the wayside.... I look at Sandro's face, who laughs and says: "But you don't do this!" It's true. This is the ideal, but I don't always do it, because I am also a sinner, and I'm not always that organized.

ADDRESS TO MEMBERS OF THE PONTIFICAL COLLEGES
AND RESIDENCES OF ROME, PAUL VI AUDIENCE HALL
MONDAY, MAY 12, 2014

Pope Francis @Pontifex • July 16, 2014

"Prayer, humility, and charity toward all are essential in the Christian life: they are the way to holiness."

OUR GOD IS A DAD TO US

It is the Spirit himself whom we received in baptism who teaches us, who spurs us to say to God: "Father" or, rather, "Abba!," which means "papa" or ["dad"]. Our God is like this: he is a dad to us.... Yet this filial relationship with God is not like a treasure that we keep in a corner of our life—it must be increased. It must be nourished every day with listening to the Word of God, with prayer, with participation in the sacraments, especially Reconciliation and the Eucharist, and with love.

GENERAL AUDIENCE, ST. PETER'S SQUARE
WEDNESDAY, APRIL 10, 2013

Pope Francis @Pontifex • October 21, 2013
"If we are to know the Lord, we must go to him. Listen to him in silence before the tabernacle and approach him in the sacraments."

GOD SPEAKS IN SACRED SCRIPTURE AND IN SILENCE
Another good way to grow in friendship with Christ is by listening to his word. The Lord speaks to us in the depths of our conscience, he speaks to us through Sacred Scripture, he speaks to us in prayer. Learn to stay before him in silence, to read and meditate on the Bible, especially the Gospels, to converse with him every day in order to feel his presence of friendship and love.

MESSAGE TO YOUNG LITHUANIANS, FROM THE VATICAN
FRIDAY, JUNE 21, 2013

Carry the Gospel in Your Pocket or Purse

We, the disciples of Jesus, are called to be people who listen to his voice and take his words seriously. To listen to Jesus, we must be close to him, to follow him, like the crowd in the Gospel who chase him through the streets of Palestine. Jesus did not have a teaching post or a fixed pulpit, he was an itinerant teacher, who proposed his teachings, teachings given to him by the Father, along the streets, covering distances that were not always predictable or easy. Follow Jesus in order to listen to him. But also let us listen to Jesus in his written Word, in the Gospel. I pose a question to you: do you read a passage of the Gospel everyday? Yes, no… yes, no… half of the time…some say yes, some no. It is important! Do you read the Gospel? It is so good; it is a good thing to have a small book of the Gospel, a little one, and to carry it in our pocket or in our purse and read a little passage in whatever moment presents itself during the day. In any given moment of the day I take the Gospel from my pocket and I read something, a short passage. Jesus is there and he speaks to us in the Gospel!

ANGELUS, ST. PETER'S SQUARE
SUNDAY, MARCH 16, 2014

RECOVER A CONTEMPLATIVE SPIRIT

The best incentive for sharing the Gospel comes from contemplating it with love, lingering over its pages and reading it with the heart. If we approach it in this way, its beauty will amaze and constantly excite us. But if this is to come about, we need to recover a contemplative spirit which can help us to realize ever anew that we have been entrusted with a treasure which makes us more human and helps us to lead a new life. There is nothing more precious which we can give to others.

APOSTOLIC EXHORTATION, *EVANGELII GAUDIUM*, 264
NOVEMBER 24, 2013

MEDITATING WITH MARY AND THE ROSARY

I would like to emphasize the beauty of a simple contemplative prayer, accessible to all, great and small, the educated and those with little education. It is the prayer of the holy rosary. In the rosary we turn to the Virgin Mary so that she may guide us to an ever closer union with her Son Jesus to bring us into conformity with him, to have his sentiments and to behave like him. Indeed, in the rosary while we repeat the Hail Mary we meditate on the mysteries, on the events of Christ's life, so as to know and love him ever better. The rosary is an effective means for opening ourselves to God, for it helps us to overcome egotism and to bring peace to our hearts, to our families, to society and to the world.

MESSAGE TO YOUNG LITHUANIANS, FROM THE VATICAN
FRIDAY, JUNE 21, 2013

Pope Francis @Pontifex • April 8, 2013

"We need to rediscover a contemplative spirit, so that the love of God may warm our hearts."

We Are All Frail and Need Help

We are human beings, marked by fragility and limitations. We are all frail, we all have limitations. Nevertheless, in these difficult moments it is necessary to trust in God's help through childlike prayer, and, at the same time, it is important to find the courage and the humility to open up to others, to ask for help, to ask for a helping hand. How often have we done this and then succeeded in emerging from our difficulty and finding God again! In this communion—communion means common-union— we form a great family, where every member is helped and sustained by the others.

GENERAL AUDIENCE, ST. PETER'S SQUARE
WEDNESDAY, OCTOBER 30, 2013

Make Room for the Lord

To avoid running aground on the rocks, our spiritual life cannot be reduced to a few religious moments. In the succession of days and seasons, in the unfolding of times and events, we learn to see ourselves by looking to the One who does not pass away: spirituality is a return to the essential, to that good that no one can take from us, the one truly necessary thing. Even in times of aridity, when pastoral situations become difficult and we have the impression that we have been left alone, it is a mantle of consolation greater than any bitterness; it is a meter of freedom from the judgment of so-called "common sense;" it is a fount of joy that enables us to receive everything from the hand of God and to contemplate his presence in everything and everyone.

Let us never tire, therefore, of seeking the Lord—of letting ourselves be sought by him—of tending over our relationship with him in silence and prayerful listening. Let us keep our gaze fixed on him, the center of time and history; let us make room for his presence within us.

ADDRESS TO MEMBERS OF THE ITALIAN EPISCOPAL
CONFERENCE, SYNOD HALL
MONDAY, MAY 19, 2014

Pope Francis @Pontifex • May 24, 2013

"Miracles happen. But prayer is needed! Prayer that is courageous, struggling and persevering, not prayer that is a mere formality."

PRAYER IS THE BREATH OF FAITH

Each one of us in our own daily lives can testify to Christ by the power of God, the power of faith. The faith we have is miniscule, but it is strong: with the power to testify to Jesus Christ, to be Christians with our life, with our witness!

And how do we draw from this strength? We draw it from God in prayer. Prayer is the breath of faith: in a relationship of trust, in a relationship of love, dialogue cannot be left out, and prayer is the dialogue of the soul with God.

ANGELUS, ST. PETER'S SQUARE
SUNDAY, OCTOBER 6, 2013

THE DANGERS OF PRIVATIZED SPIRITUALITY

Without prolonged moments of adoration, of prayerful encounter with the word, of sincere conversation with the Lord, our work easily becomes meaningless; we lose energy as a result of weariness and difficulties, and our fervor dies out. The Church urgently needs the deep breath of prayer, and to my great joy groups devoted to prayer and intercession, the prayerful reading of God's word and the perpetual adoration of the Eucharist are growing at every level of ecclesial life. Even so, "we must reject the temptation to offer a privatized and individualistic spirituality which ill accords with the demands of charity, to say nothing of the implications of the incarnation." There is always the risk that some moments of prayer can become an excuse for not offering one's life in mission; a privatized lifestyle can lead Christians to take refuge in some false forms of spirituality.

APOSTOLIC EXHORTATION, *EVANGELII GAUDIUM*, 262
NOVEMBER 24, 2013

SHARE THE GRACE YOU RECEIVE

From the event of the Transfiguration I would like to take two significant elements that can be summed up in two words: ascent and descent. We all need to go apart, to ascend the mountain in a space of silence, to find ourselves and better perceive the voice of the Lord. This we do in prayer. But we cannot stay there! Encounter with God in prayer inspires us anew to "descend the mountain" and return to the plain where we meet many brothers weighed down by fatigue, sickness, injustice, ignorance, poverty both material and spiritual. To these brothers in difficulty, we are called to bear the fruit of that experience with God, by sharing the grace we have received. And this is curious. When we hear the Word of Jesus, when we listen to the Word of Jesus and carry it in our heart, this Word grows. Do you know how it grows? By giving it to the other! The Word of Christ grows in us when we proclaim it, when we give it to others! And this is what Christian life is. It is a mission for the whole Church, for all the baptized, for us all: listen to Jesus and offer him to others. Do not forget: this week listen to Jesus!

ANGELUS, ST. PETER'S SQUARE
SUNDAY, MARCH 16, 2014

CHAPTER FIVE

~ Discover True Joy ~

[Francis of Assisi] insisted that spiritual joy was an infallible remedy against a thousand snares and tricks of the enemy. He used to say, "The devil is most delighted when he can steal the joy of spirit from a servant of God. He carries dust which he tries to throw into the tiniest openings of the conscience, to dirty a clear mind and a clean life. But if spiritual joy fills the heart, the serpent casts its poison in vain. The devils cannot harm a servant of Christ when they see him filled with holy cheerfulness. But when the spirit is teary-eyed, feeling abandoned and sad, it will easily be swallowed up in sorrow, or else be carried away toward empty enjoyment." The saint therefore always strove to keep a joyful heart, to preserve the anointing of the spirit and the oil of gladness.[5]

— THOMAS OF CELANO,
The Second Life of Saint Francis

5. *Trilogy*, p. 247.

A Joy No One Can Take Away

Christian joy, like hope, is founded on God's fidelity, on the certainty that he always keeps his promises. The Prophet Isaiah exhorts those who have lost their way and have lost heart to entrust themselves to the faithfulness of the Lord, for his salvation will not delay in bursting into their lives. All those who have encountered Jesus along the way experience a serenity and joy in their hearts which nothing and no one can take away. Our joy is Jesus Christ, his faithful love is inexhaustible!

ANGELUS, ST. PETER'S SQUARE
SUNDAY, DECEMBER 15, 2013

Pope Francis @Pontifex • March 7, 2014

"Our deepest joy comes from Christ: remaining with him, walking with him, being his disciples."

In the Footsteps of St. Francis

In the eyes of God we are the most beautiful thing, the greatest, the best of creation: even the angels are beneath us; we are more than the angels, as we heard in the Book of Psalms. The Lord favors us! We must give thanks to him for this. The gift of knowledge sets us in profound harmony with the Creator and allows us to participate in the clarity of his vision and his judgment. And it is in this perspective that we manage to accept man and woman as the summit of creation, as the fulfillment of a plan of love that is impressed in each one of us and that allows us to recognize one another as brothers and sisters.

All this is a source of serenity and peace and makes the Christian a joyful witness of God, in the footsteps of St. Francis of Assisi and so many Saints who knew how to praise and laud his love through the contemplation of creation.

GENERAL AUDIENCE, ST. PETER'S SQUARE
WEDNESDAY, MAY 21, 2014

WITH CHRIST, JOY IS BORN ANEW

The joy of the gospel fills the hearts and lives of all who encounter Jesus. Those who accept his offer of salvation are set free from sin, sorrow, inner emptiness and loneliness. With Christ, joy is constantly born anew.

APOSTOLIC EXHORTATION, *EVANGELII GAUDIUM,* 1
NOVEMBER 24, 2013

A Joy Full of Wonder

The dominant sentiment that shines forth from the Gospel accounts of the Resurrection is joy full of wonder, but a great wonder! Joy that comes from within! And in the liturgy we relive the state of mind of the disciples over the news which the women had brought: Jesus is Risen! We have seen him!

Let us allow this experience which is inscribed in the Gospel also to be imprinted in our hearts and shine forth from our lives. Let us allow the joyous wonder of Easter Sunday to shine forth in our thoughts, glances, behavior, gestures and words.... If only we were so luminous! But this is not just cosmetic! It comes from within, from a heart immersed in the source of this joy.

REGINA CAELI, ST. PETER'S SQUARE
EASTER MONDAY, APRIL 21, 2014

TRUE JOY REMAINS AMID OUR TRIALS

The joy of the Gospel is not just any joy. It consists in knowing one is welcomed and loved by God.... And so we are able to open our eyes again, to overcome sadness and mourning to strike up a new song. And this true joy remains even amid trial, even amid suffering, for it is not a superficial joy: it permeates the depths of the person who entrusts himself to the Lord and confides in him.

ANGELUS, ST. PETER'S SQUARE
SUNDAY, DECEMBER 15, 2013

Pope Francis @Pontifex • July 2, 2013

"We cannot live as Christians separate from the rock who is Christ. He gives us strength and stability, but also joy and serenity."

A REMEDY FOR SADNESS

Dear brothers and sisters, the Word of God and the
Eucharist fill us with joy always. Remember it well! When
you are sad, take up the Word of God. When you are down,
take up the Word of God and go to Sunday Mass and
receive Communion, to participate in the mystery of Jesus.
The Word of God, the Eucharist: they fill us with joy.

REGINA CAELI, ST. PETER'S SQUARE
SUNDAY, MAY 4, 2014

THE GIFT OF JOY

Read the Gospel. Read the Gospel. We have spoken about it, do you remember? To read a passage of the Gospel every day; and to carry a little Gospel with us, in our pocket, in a purse, in some way, to keep it at hand. And there, reading a passage, we will find Jesus. Everything takes on meaning when you find your treasure there, in the Gospel. Jesus calls it "the Kingdom of God," that is to say, God who reigns in your life, in our life; God who is love, peace and joy in every man and in all men. This is what God wants and it is why Jesus gave himself up to death on the cross, to free us from the power of darkness and to move us to the kingdom of life, of beauty, of goodness and of joy. To read the Gospel is to find Jesus and to have this Christian joy, which is a gift of the Holy Spirit.

Dear brothers and sisters, the joy of finding the treasure of the Kingdom of God shines through, it's visible. The Christian cannot keep his faith hidden, because it shines through in every word, in every deed, even the most simple and mundane: the love that God has given through Jesus shines through.

ANGELUS, ST. PETER'S SQUARE
SUNDAY, JULY 27, 2014

Pope Francis @Pontifex • February 4, 2014

"Dear young people, Jesus gives us life, life in abundance. If we are close to him we will have joy in our hearts and a smile on our face."

A QUIET YET FIRM TRUST

There are Christians whose lives seem like Lent without Easter. I realize of course that joy is not expressed the same way at all times in life, especially at moments of great difficulty. Joy adapts and changes, but it always endures, even as a flicker of light born of our personal certainty that, when everything is said and done, we are infinitely loved. I understand the grief of people who have to endure great suffering, yet slowly but surely we all have to let the joy of faith slowly revive as a quiet yet firm trust, even amid the greatest distress.

APOSTOLIC EXHORTATION, *EVANGELII GAUDIUM,* 6
NOVEMBER 24, 2013

True Joy Is Contagious

Joy, true joy, is contagious; it is infectious…it impels one forward….There is no holiness in sadness, there isn't any! St. Teresa—there are many Spaniards here and they know it well—said: "a Saint who is sad is a sad Saint"…When you see a seminarian, a priest, a sister or a novice with a long face, gloomy, who seems to have thrown a soaking wet blanket over their life, one of those heavy blankets… which pulls one down….Something has gone wrong! But please: never any sisters, never any priests with faces like pickled chili peppers!

ADDRESS TO SEMINARIANS AND NOVICES,
PAUL VI AUDIENCE HALL
SATURDAY, JULY 6, 2013

The Lord Will Never Abandon Us

It is always a joyful experience for us to read and reflect on the Beatitudes!… In proclaiming the Beatitudes, Jesus asks us to follow him and to travel with him along the path of love, the path that alone leads to eternal life. It is not an easy journey, yet the Lord promises us his grace and he never abandons us. We face so many challenges in life: poverty, distress, humiliation, the struggle for justice, persecutions, the difficulty of daily conversion, the effort to remain faithful to our call to holiness, and many others. But if we open the door to Jesus and allow him to be part of our lives, if we share our joys and sorrows with him, then we will experience the peace and joy that only God, who is infinite love, can give.

MESSAGE FOR THE 29TH WORLD YOUTH DAY,
FROM THE VATICAN
TUESDAY, JANUARY 21, 2014

Pope Francis @Pontifex • July 10, 2013
"If we wish to follow Christ closely, we cannot choose an easy, quiet life. It will be a demanding life, but full of joy."

Christians Cannot Be Pessimists!

Dear friends, if we walk in hope, allowing ourselves to be surprised by the new wine which Jesus offers us, we have joy in our hearts and we cannot fail to be witnesses of this joy. Christians are joyful, they are never gloomy. God is at our side.... Sin and death have been defeated. Christians cannot be pessimists! They do not look like someone in constant mourning. If we are truly in love with Christ and if we sense how much he loves us, our heart will "light up" with a joy that spreads to everyone around us.

HOMILY, 28TH WORLD YOUTH DAY,
SHRINE OF OUR LADY OF APARECIDA, BRAZIL
WEDNESDAY, JULY 24, 2013

Do Not Be Sourpusses

One of the more serious temptations which stifles boldness and zeal is a defeatism which turns us into querulous and disillusioned pessimists, "sourpusses." Nobody can go off to battle unless he is fully convinced of victory beforehand. If we start without confidence, we have already lost half the battle and we bury our talents. While painfully aware of our own frailties, we have to march on without giving in, keeping in mind what the Lord said to St. Paul: "My grace is sufficient for you, for my power is made perfect in weakness" (2 Cor 12:9).

APOSTOLIC EXHORTATION, *EVANGELII GAUDIUM*, 85
NOVEMBER 24, 2013

How Horrible is a Sad Bishop!

Your families and local communities have passed on to you the great gift of faith; Christ has grown in you. Today he desires to come here to confirm you in this faith, faith in the living Christ who dwells within you, but I have come as well to be confirmed by the enthusiasm of your faith! You know that in the life of a bishop there are many problems that need to be resolved. And with these problems and difficulties, a bishop's faith can grow sad. How horrible is a sad bishop! How bad is that! So that my faith might not be sad, I came here to be filled with your contagious enthusiasm!

WELCOMING CEREMONY, 28TH WORLD YOUTH DAY,
RIO DE JANEIRO
FRIDAY, JULY 26, 2013

Pope Francis @Pontifex • January 30, 2014
"I cannot imagine a Christian who does not know how to smile. May we joyfully witness to our faith."

SUPERFICIAL JOY AND LASTING JOY

I wanted to say a word to you and the word is "joy." Wherever there are consecrated people, seminarians, men and women religious and young people, there is joy, there is always joy! It is the joy of freshness, the joy of following Jesus; the joy that the Holy Spirit gives us, not the joy of the world....

Some will say: joy is born from possessions, so they go in quest of the latest model of the Smartphone, the fastest scooter, the showy car.... But I tell you, it truly grieves me to see a priest or a sister with the latest model of a car: but this can't be! It can't be. You think: "So do we now have to go by bicycle, Father?" Bicycles are good! Monsignor Alfred rides a bicycle. He goes by bike. I think that cars are necessary because there is so much work to be done, and also in order to get about…but choose a more humble car! And if you like the beautiful one, only think of all the children who are dying of hunger. That's all! Joy is not born from, does not come from things we possess!… Joy is born from the grace of an encounter!

ADDRESS TO SEMINARIANS AND NOVICES,
PAUL VI AUDIENCE HALL
SATURDAY, JULY 6, 2013

THE DANGERS OF CONSUMERISM

The great danger in today's world, pervaded as it is by consumerism, is the desolation and anguish born of a complacent yet covetous heart, the feverish pursuit of frivolous pleasures, and a blunted conscience. Whenever our interior life becomes caught up in its own interests and concerns, there is no longer room for others, no place for the poor. God's voice is no longer heard, the quiet joy of his love is no longer felt, and the desire to do good fades. This is a very real danger for believers too. Many fall prey to it, and end up resentful, angry and listless. That is no way to live a dignified and fulfilled life; it is not God's will for us, nor is it the life in the Spirit which has its source in the heart of the risen Christ.

APOSTOLIC EXHORTATION, *EVANGELII GAUDIUM,* 2
NOVEMBER 24, 2013

You Have Been Entrusted with a Great Duty

Our technological society—Paul VI already said it—multiplies *ad infinitum* the opportunities for pleasure, distraction, curiosity, but it cannot lead man to true joy. So much convenience, so many beautiful things, but where is the joy? In order to love life we don't need to fill it up with things, which then become idols; we need only that Jesus watch over us. It is his gaze that tells us: it is good that you are alive, your life is not useless, because you have been entrusted with a great duty. This is true wisdom: a new outlook on life that comes from an encounter with Jesus.

ADDRESS TO PARTICIPANTS OF
ROME DIOCESAN CONFERENCE
MONDAY, JUNE 16, 2014

ABBA, MAKE US JOYFUL WITNESSES!

Dear friends, in the Letter to the Romans the Apostle Paul states: "For all who are led by the Spirit of God are sons of God. For you did not receive the spirit of slavery to fall back into fear, but you have received the spirit of sonship," from which, "we cry, 'Abba! Father!'" (Rm 8:14–15). Let us ask the Lord for the gift of his Spirit to conquer our fear, our uncertainty, and our restless, impatient spirit. And let us ask him to make us joyful witnesses of God and of his love, by worshipping the Lord in truth and in service to our neighbor with gentleness and with a smile, which the Holy Spirit always gives us in joy.

GENERAL AUDIENCE, ST. PETER'S SQUARE
WEDNESDAY, JUNE 4, 2014

CHAPTER SIX

~ Choose Simplicity and Humility ~

Pure and holy Simplicity
puts all the learning of this world,
all natural wisdom, to shame.
Holy Poverty
puts to shame all greed, avarice,
and all the anxieties of this life.
Holy Humility
puts pride to shame,
and all the inhabitants of this world
and all that is in the world.[6]

—FRANCIS OF ASSISI,
"The Praises of the Virtues"

6. *Omnibus*, p. 132.

THE COURAGE TO LIVE SIMPLY

Try to be free with regard to material things. The Lord calls us to a Gospel lifestyle marked by sobriety, by a refusal to yield to the culture of consumerism. This means being concerned with the essentials and learning to do without all those unneeded extras which hem us in. Let us learn to be detached from possessiveness and from the idolatry of money and lavish spending. Let us put Jesus first. He can free us from the kinds of idol-worship which enslave us. Put your trust in God, dear young friends! He knows and loves us, and he never forgets us. Just as he provides for the lilies of the field (cf. Mt 6:28), so he will make sure that we lack nothing. If we are to come through the financial crisis, we must be also ready to change our lifestyle and avoid so much wastefulness. Just as we need the courage to be happy, we also need the courage to live simply.

MESSAGE FOR THE 29TH WORLD YOUTH DAY,
FROM THE VATICAN
TUESDAY, JANUARY 21, 2014

LEARN FROM JESUS, GENTLE AND LOWLY OF HEART

Jesus promises to give rest to everyone, but he also gives us an invitation, which is like a commandment: "Take my yoke upon you, and learn from me; for I am gentle and lowly in heart" (Mt 11:29). The "yoke" of the Lord consists in taking on the burden of others with fraternal love. Once Christ's comfort and rest is received, we are called in turn to become rest and comfort for our brothers and sisters, with a docile and humble attitude, in imitation of the Teacher. Docility and humility of heart help us not only to take on the burden of others, but also to keep our personal views, our judgments, our criticism or our indifference from weighing on them.

ANGELUS, ST. PETER'S SQUARE
SUNDAY, JULY 6, 2014

Pope Francis @Pontifex • August 7, 2014

"The Christian is someone who can decrease so that the Lord may increase, in his heart and in the heart of others."

What It Means to Be "Blessed"

The Beatitudes of Jesus are new. In fact, they are revolutionary. They present a model of happiness contrary to the logic of this world. Those whom Jesus proclaimed blessed are regarded as useless, or "losers." What the world glorifies is success at any cost, affluence, the arrogance of power and self-affirmation at the expense of others. Jesus offers a different definition of what it means to be "blessed;" he shows us the way to life and happiness, the way that he himself has taken. In fact, Jesus himself is the way!

MESSAGE TO DUTCH YOUNG PEOPLE, FROM THE VATICAN
SATURDAY, JUNE 28, 2014

Pope Francis @Pontifex • July 24, 2014

"When one lives attached to money, pride or power, it is impossible to be truly happy."

"Rosewater" Christians

This is how it is with the Kingdom of God: those who find it have no doubts, they sense that this is what they have been seeking and waiting for; and this is what fulfills their most authentic aspirations. And it really is like this: those who know Jesus and encounter him personally—are captivated, attracted by so much goodness, so much truth, so much beauty—and all with great humility and simplicity. To seek Jesus, to find Jesus: this is the great treasure!

Many people, many saints, reading the Gospel with an open heart, have been so struck by Jesus they convert to Him. Let us think of St. Francis of Assisi: he was already a Christian, though a "rosewater" Christian. When he read the Gospel, in that decisive moment of his youth, he encountered Jesus and discovered the Kingdom of God; with this, all his dreams of worldly glory vanished. The Gospel allows you to know the real Jesus, it lets you know the living Jesus; it speaks to your heart and changes your life.

ANGELUS, ST. PETER'S SQUARE
SUNDAY, JULY 27, 2014

No One is Too Small, Each Has a Role

If we read Chapter 12 of St. Paul's First Letter to the Corinthians we see that there is neither great nor small: each fulfills a role, the help he gives the others.... No one needs to feel that he is small, too small compared with someone too great. We are all little in the sight of God, in Christian humility, but we all have a role. Everyone! Like in the Church.... Who is more important in the Church? The pope or that old lady who prays the rosary every day for the Church? Only God can say: I cannot say. But everyone is important to this harmony, because the Church is the harmony of diversity. The body of Christ is this harmony in diversity, and the One who creates this harmony is the Holy Spirit: the Holy Spirit is the most important of all. This is what you said, and I wish to emphasize it. It is important: to seek unity and not to follow the logic that the big fish swallows the little one.

ADDRESS TO MEMBERS OF THE "CORALLO" ASSOCIATION,
CLEMENTINE HALL
SATURDAY, MARCH 22, 2014

Mary's Strength and Humility

Whenever we look to Mary, we come to believe once again in the revolutionary nature of love and tenderness. In her we see that humility and tenderness are not virtues of the weak but of the strong who need not treat others poorly in order to feel important themselves. Contemplating Mary, we realize that she who praised God for "bringing down the mighty from their thrones" and "sending the rich away empty" (Lk 1:52–53) is also the one who brings a homely warmth to our pursuit of justice.

APOSTOLIC EXHORTATION, *EVANGELII GAUDIUM*, 288
NOVEMBER 24, 2013

IMITATING CHRIST AND ST. FRANCIS

Let us try to understand what it means to be "poor in spirit." When the Son of God became man, he chose the path of poverty and self-emptying. As St. Paul said in his letter to the Philippians: "Let the same mind be in you that was in Christ Jesus, who, though he was in the form of God, did not count equality with God a thing to be grasped, but emptied himself, taking the form of a servant, being born in human likeness" (2:5–7). Jesus is God who strips himself of his glory....

Saint Francis of Assisi understood perfectly the secret of the Beatitude of the poor in spirit. Indeed, when Jesus spoke to him through the leper and from the crucifix, Francis recognized both God's grandeur and his own lowliness. In his prayer, the Poor Man of Assisi would spend hours asking the Lord: "Who are you?" "Who am I?" He renounced an affluent and carefree life in order to marry "Lady Poverty," to imitate Jesus and to follow the Gospel to the letter. Francis lived in imitation of Christ in his poverty and in love for the poor—for him the two were inextricably linked—like two sides of one coin.

MESSAGE FOR THE 29TH WORLD YOUTH DAY,
FROM THE VATICAN
TUESDAY, JANUARY 21, 2014

Pope Francis @Pontifex • April 24, 2014

"A simple lifestyle is good for us, helping us to better share with those in need."

PUT CHRIST FIRST

The renunciation of St. Francis tells us simply what the Gospel teaches: following Jesus means putting him in first place, stripping ourselves of the many things that we possess that suffocate our hearts, renouncing ourselves, taking up the cross and carrying it with Jesus. Stripping ourselves of prideful ego and detaching ourselves from the desire to possess, from money, which is an idol that possesses.

MEETING WITH THE POOR ASSISTED BY CARITAS,
ARCHBISHOP'S RESIDENCE, ASSISI
FRIDAY, OCTOBER 4, 2013

Pope Francis @Pontifex • August 5, 2014

"If you hoard material possessions, they will rob you of your soul."

THE CULTURE OF PROSPERITY DEADENS US

To sustain a lifestyle which excludes others, or to sustain enthusiasm for that selfish ideal, a globalization of indifference has developed. Almost without being aware of it, we end up being incapable of feeling compassion at the outcry of the poor, weeping for other people's pain, and feeling a need to help them, as though all this were someone else's responsibility and not our own. The culture of prosperity deadens us; we are thrilled if the market offers us something new to purchase. In the meantime all those lives stunted for lack of opportunity seem a mere spectacle; they fail to move us.

APOSTOLIC EXHORTATION, *EVANGELII GAUDIUM*, 54
NOVEMBER 24, 2013

To Touch the Poor and Humble Is to Touch Christ

Theoretical poverty is not needed, but rather the poverty that we learn by touching the flesh of the poor Christ, in the humble, in the poor, in the sick, in children. Still, today may you be, for the Church and for the world, the outposts of care for all the poor and for all material, moral and spiritual poverty. May you be examples in overcoming every form of egoism through the logic of the Gospel which teaches us to trust in the Providence of God.

MESSAGE, SYMPOSIUM ON THE MANAGEMENT OF
ECCLESIASTICAL GOODS,
PONTIFICAL ANTONIANUM UNIVERSITY
SATURDAY, MARCH 8, 2014

Pope Francis @Pontifex • June 2, 2013

"The world tells us to seek success, power and money; God tells us to seek humility, service and love."

NO ONE IS EXEMPT FROM CONCERN FOR THE POOR

No one must say that they cannot be close to the poor because their own lifestyle demands more attention to other areas. This is an excuse commonly heard in academic, business or professional, and even ecclesial circles. While it is quite true that the essential vocation and mission of the lay faithful is to strive that earthly realities and all human activity may be transformed by the Gospel, none of us can think we are exempt from concern for the poor and for social justice: "Spiritual conversion, the intensity of the love of God and neighbor, zeal for justice and peace, the Gospel meaning of the poor and of poverty, are required of everyone." I fear that these words too may give rise to commentary or discussion with no real practical effect. That being said, I trust in the openness and readiness of all Christians, and I ask you to seek, as a community, creative ways of accepting this renewed call.

APOSTOLIC EXHORTATION, *EVANGELII GAUDIUM*, 201
NOVEMBER 24, 2013

Pope Francis @Pontifex • July 19, 2014

"The Lord loves a cheerful giver. May we learn to be generous in giving, free from the love of material possessions."

CHRIST'S FACE IN THE POOR AND OUTCAST

In the poor and outcast we see Christ's face; by loving and helping the poor, we love and serve Christ. Our efforts are also directed to ending violations of human dignity, discrimination and abuse in the world, for these are so often the cause of destitution. When power, luxury and money become idols, they take priority over the need for a fair distribution of wealth. Our consciences thus need to be converted to justice, equality, simplicity and sharing.

2014 LENTEN MESSAGE, FROM THE VATICAN
THURSDAY, DECEMBER 26, 2013

EVANGELICAL POVERTY AND EFFECTIVE EVANGELIZATION

There is a close connection between poverty and evangelization, between the theme of the last World Youth Day—"Go therefore, and make disciples of all nations!" (Mt 28:19)—and the theme for this year: "Blessed are the poor in spirit, for theirs is the kingdom of heaven" (Mt 5:3). The Lord wants a poor Church which evangelizes the poor. When Jesus sent the Twelve out on mission, he said to them: "Take no gold, nor silver, nor copper in your belts, no bag for your journey, nor two tunics, nor sandals, nor a staff; for the laborers deserve their food" (Mt 10:9–10). Evangelical poverty is a basic condition for spreading the kingdom of God.

MESSAGE FOR THE 29TH WORLD YOUTH DAY,
FROM THE VATICAN
TUESDAY, JANUARY 21, 2014

Pope Francis @Pontifex • August 2, 2014

"When we do not adore God, we adore something else. Money and power are false idols which often take the place of God."

TRUE POWER IS FOUND IN SERVICE, HUMILITY, LOVE

We must never forget that true power, at any level, is service, whose bright summit is upon the Cross. Benedict XVI, with great wisdom, often reminded the Church that although man frequently equates authority with control, dominion, success, for God authority is always synonymous with service, humility, love; it means entering the logic of Jesus who kneels to wash the Apostles' feet and says to his disciples.... (cf Mt 20:25–17).

Let us think of the damage done to the People of God by men and women of the Church who are careerists, climbers, who "use" the People, the Church, our brothers and sisters—those they should be serving—as a springboard for their own ends and personal ambitions. These people do the Church great harm.

ADDRESS TO THE INTERNATIONAL UNION OF
SUPERIORS GENERAL, PAUL VI AUDIENCE HALL
WEDNESDAY, MAY 8, 2013

Pope Francis @Pontifex • June 12, 2013

"How many kinds of moral and material poverty we face today as a result of denying God and putting so many idols in his place!"

MOTHER OF GOD, STRENGTHEN US IN OUR MISSION! The Mother of the Redeemer goes before us and continually strengthens us in faith, in our vocation and in our mission. By her example of humility and openness to God's will she helps us to transmit our faith in a joyful proclamation of the Gospel to all, without reservation. In this way our mission will be fruitful, because it is modeled on the motherhood of Mary. To her let us entrust our journey of faith, the desires of our heart, our needs and the needs of the whole world, especially of those who hunger and thirst for justice and peace, and for God. Let us then together invoke her. I invite you to invoke her three times, following the example of those brothers and sisters of Ephesus: Mother of God! Mother of God! Mother of God! Amen.

HOMILY, ST. PETER'S BASILICA
SOLEMNITY OF MARY, MOTHER OF GOD,
WEDNESDAY, JANUARY 1, 2014

CHAPTER SEVEN

~ Do Not Forget the Poor! ~

Francis, conforming himself to the poor in all things, was distressed to see anyone poorer than himself, not out of any desire for empty glory, but from a feeling of simple compassion. Though he was content with a rough tunic, he often wished to divide it with some poor person....

A certain brother insulted a poor man begging alms, saying: "Are you sure that you are not really rich and just pretending to be poor?" When Saint Francis heard this, he rebuked the brother who had said these things.... He used to say: "Anyone who curses the poor insults Christ whose noble banner the poor carry, since Christ made himself poor for us in this world." That is also why, when he met poor people burdened with wood or other heavy loads, he would offer his own weak shoulders to help them.[7]

—THOMAS OF CELANO,
First Life of St. Francis

7. Trilogy, pp. 87–88.

Why I Chose the Name Francis

As you know, there are various reasons why I chose the name of Francis of Assisi, a familiar figure far beyond the borders of Italy and Europe, even among those who do not profess the Catholic faith. One of the first reasons was Francis' love for the poor. How many poor people there still are in the world! And what great suffering they have to endure! After the example of Francis of Assisi, the Church in every corner of the globe has always tried to care for and look after those who suffer from want, and I think that in many of your countries you can attest to the generous activity of Christians who dedicate themselves to helping the sick, orphans, the homeless and all the marginalized, thus striving to make society more humane and more just.

ADDRESS TO THE DIPLOMATIC CORPS ACCREDITED TO
THE HOLY SEE, SALA REGIA
FRIDAY, MARCH 22, 2013

Let Us Go Out to Meet the Poor!

All of us need to experience a conversion in the way we see the poor. We have to care for them and be sensitive to their spiritual and material needs. To you young people I especially entrust the task of restoring solidarity to the heart of human culture. Faced with old and new forms of poverty—unemployment, migration and addictions of various kinds—we have the duty to be alert and thoughtful, avoiding the temptation to remain indifferent. We have to remember all those who feel unloved, who have no hope for the future and who have given up on life out of discouragement, disappointment or fear. We have to learn to be on the side of the poor, and not just indulge in rhetoric about the poor! Let us go out to meet them, look into their eyes and listen to them. The poor provide us with a concrete opportunity to encounter Christ himself, and to touch his suffering flesh.

MESSAGE FOR THE 29TH WORLD YOUTH DAY,
FROM THE VATICAN
TUESDAY, JANUARY 21, 2014

Pope Francis @Pontifex • August 23, 2013

"Lord, teach us to step outside ourselves. Teach us to go out into the streets and manifest your love."

WE ARE CALLED TO BE FRIENDS WITH THE POOR

This is why I want a Church which is poor and for the poor. They have much to teach us. Not only do they share in the sensus fidei, but in their difficulties they know the suffering Christ. We need to let ourselves be evangelized by them. The new evangelization is an invitation to acknowledge the saving power at work in their lives and to put them at the center of the Church's pilgrim way. We are called to find Christ in them, to lend our voice to their causes, but also to be their friends, to listen to them, to speak for them and to embrace the mysterious wisdom which God wishes to share with us through them.

APOSTOLIC EXHORTATION, *EVANGELII GAUDIUM*, 198
NOVEMBER 24, 2013

COMPASSION IS NOT SIMPLY FEELING PITY

This Sunday, the Gospel presents to us the miracle of the multiplication of loaves and fish (Mt 14:13–21)....

In facing the crowd who follows him and—so to speak— "won't leave him alone," Jesus does not react with irritation; he does not say: "These people are bothering me." No, no. He reacts with a feeling of compassion, because he knows they are not seeking him out of curiosity but out of need. But attention: compassion—which Jesus feels—is not simply feeling pity; it's more! It means to suffer with, in other words to empathize with the suffering of another, to the point of taking it upon oneself. Jesus is like this: he suffers together with us, he suffers with us, he suffers for us. And the sign of this compassion is the healing of countless people he performed. Jesus teaches us to place the needs of the poor before our own. Our needs, even if legitimate, are not as urgent as those of the poor, who lack the basic necessities of life.

ANGELUS, ST. PETER'S SQUARE
SUNDAY, AUGUST 3, 2014

In Imitation of Our Master

In imitation of our Master, we Christians are called to confront the poverty of our brothers and sisters, to touch it, to make it our own and to take practical steps to alleviate it.... In the poor and outcast we see Christ's face; by loving and helping the poor, we love and serve Christ. Our efforts are also directed to ending violations of human dignity, discrimination and abuse in the world, for these are so often the cause of destitution. When power, luxury and money become idols, they take priority over the need for a fair distribution of wealth. Our consciences thus need to be converted to justice, equality, simplicity and sharing.

2014 LENTEN MESSAGE, FROM THE VATICAN
THURSDAY, DECEMBER 26, 2013

Pope Francis @Pontifex • December 9, 2013
"If we see someone who needs help, do we stop? There is so much suffering and poverty, and a great need for good Samaritans."

Authentic Disciples

When Saint Paul approached the apostles in Jerusalem to discern whether he was "running or had run in vain" (Gal 2:2), the key criterion of authenticity which they presented was that he should not forget the poor (cf. Gal 2:10). This important principle, namely that the Pauline communities should not succumb to the self-centered lifestyle of the pagans, remains timely today, when a new self-centered paganism is growing. We may not always be able to reflect adequately the beauty of the Gospel, but there is one sign which we should never lack: the option for those who are least, those whom society discards.

APOSTOLIC EXHORTATION, *EVANGELII GAUDIUM*, 195
NOVEMBER 24, 2013

You Cannot Serve Two Masters

You cannot serve two masters: God and wealth. As long as everyone seeks to accumulate for themselves, there will never be justice. We must take heed of this! As long as everyone seeks to accumulate for themselves, there will be no justice. Instead, by entrusting ourselves to God's providence, and seeking his Kingdom together, no one will lack the necessary means to live with dignity.

ANGELUS, ST. PETER'S SQUARE
SUNDAY, MARCH 2, 2014

I Distrust a Charity That Costs Nothing

We would do well to ask ourselves what we can give up in order to help and enrich others by our own poverty. Let us not forget that real poverty hurts: no self-denial is real without this dimension of penance. I distrust a charity that costs nothing and does not hurt.

2014 LENTEN MESSAGE, FROM THE VATICAN
THURSDAY, DECEMBER 26, 2013

WE MUST CREATE A CULTURE OF ENCOUNTER

I sometimes ask people: "Do you give alms?"

They say to me: "Yes, Father."

"And when you give alms, do you look the person you are giving them to in the eye?"

"Oh, I don't know, I don't really notice."

"Then you have not really encountered him. You tossed him the alms and walked off. When you give alms, do you touch the person's hand or do you throw the coin?"

"No, I throw the coin."

"So you did not touch him. And if you don't touch him you don't meet him."

What Jesus teaches us first of all is to meet each other, and in meeting to offer each other help. We must know how to meet each other. We must build, create, construct a culture of encounter. As the theme says: "Let us meet with the most destitute," in other words with those who are needier than I am. With those who are going through a bad moment that is worse than the one that I'm going through. There is always someone worse off, isn't there? Always!

MESSAGE TO THE FAITHFUL OF BUENOS AIRES,
FROM THE VATICAN, FEAST OF SAINT CAJETAN,
WEDNESDAY, AUGUST 7, 2013

The Inclusion of the Poor in Society

Our faith in Christ, who became poor, and was always close to the poor and the outcast, is the basis of our concern for the integral development of society's most neglected members.

In union with God, we hear a plea:

Each individual Christian and every community is called to be an instrument of God for the liberation and promotion of the poor, and for enabling them to be fully a part of society. This demands that we be docile and attentive to the cry of the poor and to come to their aid.... The old question always returns: "How does God's love abide in anyone who has the world's goods, and sees a brother or sister in need and yet refuses help?" (1 Jn 3:17). Let us recall also how bluntly the apostle James speaks of the cry of the oppressed: "The wages of the laborers who mowed your fields, which you kept back by fraud, cry out, and the cries of the harvesters have reached the ears of the Lord of hosts" (5:4).

APOSTOLIC EXHORTATION,
EVANGELII GAUDIUM, 186–187
NOVEMBER 24, 2013

TRUE CHARITY DEMANDS JUSTICE

It is not enough to offer someone a sandwich unless it is accompanied by the possibility of learning how to stand on one's own two feet. Charity that leaves the poor person as he is, is not sufficient. True mercy, the mercy God gives to us and teaches us, demands justice, it demands that the poor find the way to be poor no longer. It asks—and it asks us, the Church, us, the City of Rome, it asks the institutions—to ensure that no one ever again stand in need of a soup kitchen, of makeshift lodgings, of a service of legal assistance in order to have his legitimate right recognized to live and to work, to be fully a person.

2014 LENTEN MESSAGE,
FROM THE VATICAN
THURSDAY, DECEMBER 226, 013

Pope Francis @Pontifex • September 21, 2013

"True charity requires courage: let us overcome the fear of getting our hands dirty so as to help those in need."

WE NEED MORE COMMUNITIES THAT
PUT LOVE INTO PRACTICE!

Dear men and women religious, your empty convents are not useful to the Church if they are turned into hotels and earn money. The empty convents do not belong to you, they are for the flesh of Christ which is what refugees are. The Lord calls us to live with greater courage and generosity, and to accept them in communities, houses and empty convents. This of course is not something simple; it requires a criterion and responsibility, but also courage. We do a great deal, but perhaps we are called to do more, firmly accepting and sharing with those whom Providence has given us to serve; overcoming the temptation of spiritual worldliness to be close to simple people and, especially, to the lowliest. We need communities with solidarity that really put love into practice!

2014 LENTEN MESSAGE,
FROM THE VATICAN
THURSDAY, DECEMBER 26, 2013

Pope Francis @Pontifex • April 26, 2014

"None of us can think we are exempt from concern for the poor and for social justice."

THERE ARE NO "DISPOSABLE LIVES"

The reconciled person sees in God the Father of all, and, as a consequence, is spurred on to live a life of fraternity open to all. In Christ, the other is welcomed and loved as a son or daughter of God, as a brother or sister, not as a stranger, much less as a rival or even an enemy. In God's family, where all are sons and daughters of the same Father, and, because they are grafted to Christ, sons and daughters in the Son, there are no "disposable lives." All men and women enjoy an equal and inviolable dignity. All are loved by God. All have been redeemed by the blood of Christ, who died on the Cross and rose for all. This is the reason why no one can remain indifferent before the lot of our brothers and sisters.

MESSAGE FOR THE CELEBRATION OF
THE WORLD DAY OF PEACE
WEDNESDAY, JANUARY 1, 2014

AN ECONOMY THAT KILLS

Just as the commandment "Thou shalt not kill" sets a clear limit in order to safeguard the value of human life, today we also have to say "thou shalt not" to an economy of exclusion and inequality. Such an economy kills. How can it be that it is not a news item when an elderly homeless person dies of exposure, but it is news when the stock market loses two points? This is a case of exclusion. Can we continue to stand by when food is thrown away while people are starving? This is a case of inequality. Today everything comes under the laws of competition and the survival of the fittest, where the powerful feed upon the powerless. As a consequence, masses of people find themselves excluded and marginalized: without work, without possibilities, without any means of escape.

APOSTOLIC EXHORTATION, *EVANGELII GAUDIUM*, 53
NOVEMBER 24, 2013

Pope Francis @Pontifex • July 25, 2013
"The measure of the greatness of a society is found in the way it treats those most in need, those who have nothing apart from their poverty."

Toward a Better World

A better world will come about only if attention is first paid to individuals; if human promotion is integral, taking account of every dimension of the person, including the spiritual; if no one is neglected, including the poor, the sick, prisoners, the needy and the stranger (cf. Mt 25:31–46); if we can prove capable of leaving behind a throwaway culture and embracing one of encounter and acceptance. Migrants and refugees are not pawns on the chessboard of humanity. They are children, women and men who leave or who are forced to leave their homes for various reasons, who share a legitimate desire for knowing and having, but above all for being more.... Every human being is a child of God! He or she bears the image of Christ! We ourselves need to see, and then to enable others to see, that migrants and refugees do not only represent a problem to be solved, but are brothers and sisters to be welcomed, respected and loved. They are an occasion that Providence gives us to help build a more just society, a more perfect democracy, a more united country, a more fraternal world and a more open and evangelical Christian community.

2014 MESSAGE FOR THE WORLD DAY OF MIGRANTS AND
REFUGEES, FROM THE VATICAN
MONDAY, AUGUST 5, 2013

Pope Francis @Pontifex • July 8, 2013

"We pray for a heart which will embrace immigrants. God will judge us upon how we have treated the most needy."

The Poor Are Our Priority

The proclamation of the Gospel is destined for the poor first of all, for those who all too often lack what they need in order to live a dignified life. To them first are proclaimed the glad tidings that God loves them with a preferential love and comes to visit them through the charitable works that disciples of Christ do in his name. Go to the poor first of all: this is the priority. At the moment of the Last Judgment, as we can read in Matthew 25, we shall all be judged on this.

ADDRESS AT THE ECCLESIAL CONVENTION,
DIOCESE OF ROME, PAUL VI AUDIENCE HALL
MONDAY, JUNE 17, 2013

AN APPEAL TO ALL PEOPLE OF GOOD WILL

I would like to make an appeal to those in possession of greater resources, to public authorities and to all people of good will who are working for social justice: never tire of working for a more just world, marked by greater solidarity! No one can remain insensitive to the inequalities that persist in the world! Everybody, according to his or her particular opportunities and responsibilities, should be able to make a personal contribution to putting an end to so many social injustices. The culture of selfishness and individualism that often prevails in our society is not, I repeat, not what builds up and leads to a more habitable world: rather, it is the culture of solidarity that does so; the culture of solidarity means seeing others not as rivals or statistics, but brothers and sisters. And we are all brothers and sisters!

ADDRESS TO THE COMMUNITY OF VARGINHA
[MANGUINHOS], RIO DE JANEIRO
THURSDAY, JULY 25, 2013

I Prefer a Church Which Is Bruised and Dirty

Let us go forth, then, let us go forth to offer everyone the life of Jesus Christ. Here I repeat for the entire Church what I have often said to the priests and laity of Buenos Aires: I prefer a Church which is bruised, hurting and dirty because it has been out on the streets, rather than a Church which is unhealthy from being confined and from clinging to its own security. I do not want a Church concerned with being at the center and then ends by being caught up in a web of obsessions and procedures. If something should rightly disturb us and trouble our consciences, it is the fact that so many of our brothers and sisters are living without the strength, light and consolation born of friendship with Jesus Christ, without a community of faith to support them, without meaning and a goal in life. More than by fear of going astray, my hope is that we will be moved by the fear of remaining shut up within structures which give us a false sense of security, within rules which make us harsh judges, within habits which make us feel safe, while at our door people are starving and Jesus does not tire of saying to us: "Give them something to eat" (Mk 6:37).

APOSTOLIC EXHORTATION, *EVANGELII GAUDIUM*, 49
NOVEMBER 24, 2013

CHAPTER EIGHT

~ Preach the Gospel at All Times ~

[Saint Francis] filled the whole earth with the Gospel of Christ, so that often in one day he made a circuit of four or five villages and even cities, preaching the kingdom of God to every one; and edifying his hearers not less by his example than by his word, he made a tongue out of his whole body.[8]

—THOMAS OF CELANO,
First Life of St. Francis, 97

8. *Omnibus*, p. 311.

First Witness, Then Words

Here in Assisi, close to the Portiuncula, I seem to hear the voice of St. Francis repeating: "The Gospel, the Gospel!" He says it to me as well; indeed, he says it to me first: Pope Francis, be a servant of the Gospel!…

The Gospel, then, this message of salvation, has two destinations that are connected: the first, to awaken faith, and this is evangelization; the second, to transform the world according to God's plan, and this is the Christian animation of society. But these are not two separate things, they form one mission: to carry the Gospel by the witness of our lives in order to transform the world!…

Let us look to Francis: he did both of these things, through the power of the one Gospel. Francis made faith grow and he renewed the Church, and at the same time he renewed society, he made it more fraternal, but he always did it with the Gospel and by his witness. Do you know what Francis once said to his brothers? He said: "Always preach the Gospel and if necessary use words!" But how? Is it possible to preach the Gospel without words? Yes! By your witness! First comes witness, then come words!

ADDRESS TO THE YOUNG PEOPLE OF UMBRIA, BASILICA
OF SAINT MARY OF THE ANGELS SQUARE, ASSISI
FRIDAY, OCTOBER 4, 2013

We Are Called to Be Heralds of Hope!

The Gospel is the real antidote to spiritual destitution: wherever we go, we are called as Christians to proclaim the liberating news that forgiveness for sins committed is possible, that God is greater than our sinfulness, that he freely loves us at all times and that we were made for communion and eternal life. The Lord asks us to be joyous heralds of this message of mercy and hope! It is thrilling to experience the joy of spreading this good news, sharing the treasure entrusted to us, consoling broken hearts and offering hope to our brothers and sisters experiencing darkness. It means following and imitating Jesus, who sought out the poor and sinners as a shepherd lovingly seeks his lost sheep. In union with Jesus, we can courageously open up new paths of evangelization and human promotion.

2014 LENTEN MESSAGE, FROM THE VATICAN
THURSDAY, DECEMBER 26, 2013

Pope Francis @Pontifex • June 19, 2014

"There is never a reason to lose hope. Jesus says: 'I am with you until the end of the world.'"

OUR WHOLE BEING SHOULD SPEAK OF GOD

In our cities and villages there are brave men and others who are timid, there are Christian missionaries and others who are asleep. And there are many who are searching, even if they do not admit it. Everyone is called, everyone is sent out. However, the place of the call is not necessarily the parish center; the moment is not necessarily a pleasant parish event. The call of God can reach us on the assembly line and in the office, in the supermarket and in the stairwell, that is, in the places of everyday life.

Speaking about God, bringing the message of God's love and salvation in Jesus Christ to men is the duty of all the baptized. And this duty involves, not only speaking with words, but in all one's actions and way of doing things. Our whole being should speak of God, even in the ordinary things. In this way witness is authentic, and thus shall it always be new and fresh in the power of the Holy Spirit.

ADDRESS TO THE BISHOPS OF AUSTRIA, "AD LIMINA" VISIT
THURSDAY, JANUARY 30, 2014

Pope Francis @Pontifex • May 30, 2014

"Every Christian can witness to God in the workplace, not only with words, but above all with an honest life."

THE GOSPEL IS TRUTH, LOVE AND BEAUTY

There are so many needy, so many needy…even people who hunger—but not for bread, they have plenty of bread—but for God! And go there, to tell this truth: Jesus Christ is the Lord and he saves you. But always go and touch the flesh of Christ! The Gospel cannot be preached purely intellectually: the Gospel is truth but it is also love and it is also beauty! And this is the joy of the Gospel! This is truly the joy of the Gospel.

ADDRESS AT THE PENTECOSTAL CHURCH OF
RECONCILIATION, CASERTA
MONDAY, JULY 28, 2014

A Cure for Our Infinite Sadness

If we succeed in expressing adequately and with beauty the essential content of the Gospel, surely this message will speak to the deepest yearnings of people's hearts…. Enthusiasm for evangelization is based on this conviction. We have a treasure of life and love which cannot deceive, and a message which cannot mislead or disappoint. It penetrates to the depths of our hearts, sustaining and ennobling us. It is a truth which is never out of date because it reaches that part of us which nothing else can reach. Our infinite sadness can only be cured by an infinite love.

APOSTOLIC EXHORTATION, *EVANGELII GAUDIUM*, 265
NOVEMBER 24, 2013

SIGNS OF CHRIST'S LIGHT AND LOVE

What is this people's mission? It is to bring the hope and salvation of God to the world: to be a sign of the love of God who calls everyone to friendship with him; to be the leaven that makes the dough rise, the salt that gives flavor and preserves from corruption, to be a light that enlightens. Look around us—it is enough to open a newspaper, as I said—we see the presence of evil, the devil is acting. However, I would like to say out loud: God is stronger! Do you believe this, that God is stronger? Let us say it together, let us say it all together: God is stronger! And do you know why he is stronger? Because he is Lord, the only Lord. And I would like to add that reality, at times dark and marked by evil, can change, if we first bring the light of the Gospel especially through our lives. If in a stadium—say the Olympic stadium in Rome or the San Lorenzo in Buenos Aires—on a dark night, if someone turns on a light, you can barely see it; but if the other 70,000 spectators turn on their own light, the whole stadium shines. Let our lives together be the one light of Christ; together we will carry the light of the Gospel to the whole of reality.

GENERAL AUDIENCE, ST. PETER'S SQUARE
WEDNESDAY, JUNE 12, 2013

Pope Francis @Pontifex • May 5, 2014

"What does 'evangelize' mean? To give witness with joy and simplicity to what we are and what we believe in."

Heralds of the Word of Life

I say to you, dear brothers and sisters: be everywhere heralds of the word of life in our neighborhoods, our workplaces and everywhere that people meet one another and develop relationships. You must go outside. I do not understand Christian communities that are shut into a parish.

ADDRESS AT THE ECCLESIAL CONVENTION,
DIOCESE OF ROME, PAUL VI AUDIENCE HALL
MONDAY, JUNE 17, 2013

A Passion for God's People

The word of God also invites us to recognize that we are a people: "Once you were no people but now you are God's people" (1 Pet 2:10). To be evangelizers of souls, we need to develop a spiritual taste for being close to people's lives and to discover that this is itself a source of greater joy. Mission is at once a passion for Jesus and a passion for his people. When we stand before Jesus crucified, we see the depth of his love which exalts and sustains us, but at the same time, unless we are blind, we begin to realize that Jesus' gaze, burning with love, expands to embrace all his people. We realize once more that he wants to make use of us to draw closer to his beloved people. He takes us from the midst of his people and he sends us to his people; without this sense of belonging we cannot understand our deepest identity.

APOSTOLIC EXHORTATION, *EVANGELII GAUDIUM*, 268
NOVEMBER 24, 2013

We Have Lost the Other 99!

I want to tell you something. There is a beautiful passage of the Gospel which tells us about the shepherd who, when he returned to the sheepfold realized that one sheep was missing. He left the 99 others and went in search of it, he went off to look for one. But brothers and sisters, we have one sheep. We have lost the other 99! We must go out, we must go out to them! In this culture—let us tell the truth—we only have one, we are a minority! And do we feel the fervor, the apostolic zeal to go out and find the other 99? This is an enormous responsibility and we must ask the Lord for the grace of generosity, and the courage and patience to go out, to go out and preach the Gospel. Ah, this is difficult. It is easier to stay at home, with that one sheep! It is easier with that sheep to comb its fleece, to stroke it…but we priests and you Christians too, everyone: the Lord wants us to be shepherds, he does not want us to fuss with combing fleeces!

ADDRESS AT THE ECCLESIAL CONVENTION, DIOCESE OF
ROME, PAUL VI AUDIENCE HALL
MONDAY, JUNE 17, 2013

Called to Be Missionaries

Seeing you all present here today, I think of the story of St. Francis of Assisi. In front of the crucifix he heard the voice of Jesus saying to him: "Francis, go, rebuild my house." The young Francis responded readily and generously to the Lord's call to rebuild his house. But which house? Slowly but surely, Francis came to realize that it was not a question of repairing a stone building, but about doing his part for the life of the Church. It was a matter of being at the service of the Church, loving her and working to make the countenance of Christ shine ever more brightly in her. Today too, as always, the Lord needs you, young people, for his Church. My friends, the Lord needs you! Today too, he is calling each of you to follow him in his Church and to be missionaries. The Lord is calling you today! Not the masses, but you, and you, and you, each one of you. Listen to what he is saying to you in your heart.

PRAYER VIGIL WITH THE YOUNG PEOPLE,
28TH WORLD YOUTH DAY,
WATERFRONT OF COPACABANA
SATURDAY, JULY 27, 2013

Pope Francis @Pontifex • March 25, 2014

"We cannot be tepid disciples. The Church needs our courage in order to give witness to truth."

TELL EVERYONE, "COME AND SEE!"

The message which Christians bring to the world is this: Jesus, Love Incarnate, died on the cross for our sins, but God the Father raised him and made him the Lord of life and death. In Jesus, love has triumphed over hatred, mercy over sinfulness, goodness over evil, truth over falsehood, life over death.

That is why we tell everyone: "Come and see!" In every human situation, marked by frailty, sin and death, the Good News is no mere matter of words, but a testimony to unconditional and faithful love: it is about leaving ourselves behind and encountering others, being close to those crushed by life's troubles, sharing with the needy, standing at the side of the sick, elderly and the outcast... "Come and see!" Love is more powerful, love gives life, love makes hope blossom in the wilderness.

URBI ET ORBI, LOGGIA OF ST. PETER'S BASILICA
EASTER SUNDAY, APRIL 20, 2014

Make a Joyful Noise!

Let me tell you what I hope will be the outcome of World Youth Day: I hope there will be noise. Here there will be noise, I'm quite sure. Here in Rio there will be plenty of noise, no doubt about that. But I want you to make yourselves heard in your dioceses, I want the noise to go out, I want the Church to go out onto the streets, I want us to resist everything worldly, everything static, everything comfortable, everything to do with clericalism, everything that might make us closed in on ourselves. The parishes, the schools, the institutions are made for going out…if they don't, they become an NGO, and the Church cannot be an NGO. May the bishops and priests forgive me if some of you create a bit of confusion afterwards. That's my advice. Thanks for whatever you can do.

ADDRESS TO THE YOUTH OF ARGENTINA,
28TH WORLD YOUTH DAY, RIO DE JANEIRO
THURSDAY, JULY 25, 2013

FEARLESS, SPIRIT-FILLED EVANGELIZERS

Spirit-filled evangelizers means evangelizers fearlessly open to the working of the Holy Spirit. At Pentecost, the Spirit made the apostles go forth from themselves and turned them into heralds of God's wondrous deeds, capable of speaking to each person in his or her own language. The Holy Spirit also grants the courage to proclaim the newness of the Gospel with boldness (*parrhesía*) in every time and place, even when it meets with opposition. Let us call upon him today, firmly rooted in prayer, for without prayer all our activity risks being fruitless and our message empty. Jesus wants evangelizers who proclaim the good news not only with words, but above all by a life transfigured by God's presence.

APOSTOLIC EXHORTATION, *EVANGELII GAUDIUM*, 259
NOVEMBER 24, 2013

Pope Francis @Pontifex • April 14, 2013

"Let us not forget: if we are to proclaim the Gospel of Jesus, our lives must bear witness to what we preach."

Do Not Bombard People with Religious Messages

Effective Christian witness is not about bombarding people with religious messages, but about our willingness to be available to others "by patiently and respectfully engaging their questions and their doubts as they advance in their search for the truth and the meaning of human existence" (Benedict XVI, Message for the 47ᵀᴴ World Communications Day, 2013). We need but recall the story of the disciples on the way to Emmaus. We have to be able to dialogue with the men and women of today, to understand their expectations, doubts and hopes, and to bring them the Gospel, Jesus Christ himself, God incarnate, who died and rose to free us from sin and death. We are challenged to be people of depth, attentive to what is happening around us and spiritually alert. To dialogue means to believe that the "other" has something worthwhile to say, and to entertain his or her point of view and perspective. Engaging in dialogue does not mean renouncing our own ideas and traditions; it means renouncing the claim that they alone are valid or absolute.

MESSAGE FOR THE 48ᵀᴴ WORLD COMMUNICATIONS DAY,
FROM THE VATICAN
MEMORIAL OF SAINT FRANCIS DE SALES,
JANUARY 24, 2014

Pope Francis @Pontifex • August 2, 2013

"The security of faith does not make us motionless or close us off, but sends us forth to bear witness and to dialogue with all people."

THE WITNESS OF ONE'S LIFE

Let us all remember this: one cannot proclaim the Gospel of Jesus without the tangible witness of one's life. Those who listen to us and observe us must be able to see in our actions what they hear from our lips, and so give glory to God!...Inconsistency on the part of pastors and the faithful between what they say and what they do, between word and manner of life, is undermining the Church's credibility.

HOMILY, BASILICA OF SAINT PAUL OUTSIDE-THE-WALLS
SUNDAY, APRIL 14, 2013

THE CHURCH ON THE STREETS OF THE DIGITAL HIGHWAY
As I have frequently observed, if a choice has to be made between a bruised Church which goes out to the streets and a Church suffering from self-absorption, I certainly prefer the first. Those "streets" are the world where people live and where they can be reached, both effectively and affectively. The digital highway is one of them, a street teeming with people who are often hurting, men and women looking for salvation or hope. By means of the internet, the Christian message can reach "to the ends of the earth" (Acts 1:8). Keeping the doors of our churches open also means keeping them open in the digital environment so that people, whatever their situation in life, can enter, and so that the Gospel can go out to reach everyone. We are called to show that the Church is the home of all.

MESSAGE FOR THE 48TH WORLD COMMUNICATIONS DAY,
FROM THE VATICAN
MEMORIAL OF SAINT FRANCIS DE SALES,
JANUARY 24, 2014

Pope Francis @Pontifex • September 23, 2013

"The Church has no other meaning and finality than to witness to Jesus. May we not forget this."

MAY WE BE STARS THAT MIRROR CHRIST'S LIGHT

Let us ask God, on behalf of the whole Church, let us ask for the joy of evangelizing, for we were "sent by Christ to reveal and communicate the love of God to all men and to all peoples" (Ad Gentes, n. 10). May the Virgin Mary help us all to be missionary-disciples, little stars that mirror his light. Let us pray too that hearts be open to receiving the proclamation, and that all men and women may be "partakers of the promise in Christ Jesus through the Gospel" (Eph 3:6).

ANGELUS, ST. PETER'S SQUARE
MONDAY, JANUARY 6, 2014

COME HOLY SPIRIT, RENEW THE CHURCH!

How I long to find the right words to stir up enthusiasm for a new chapter of evangelization full of fervor, joy, generosity, courage, boundless love and attraction! Yet I realize that no words of encouragement will be enough unless the fire of the Holy Spirit burns in our hearts. A spirit-filled evangelization is one guided by the Holy Spirit, for he is the soul of the Church called to proclaim the Gospel.... I once more invoke the Holy Spirit. I implore him to come and renew the Church, to stir and impel her to go forth boldly to evangelize all peoples.

APOSTOLIC EXHORTATION, *EVANGELII GAUDIUM*, 261
NOVEMBER 24, 2013

CHAPTER NINE

~ Be Instruments of Peace and Pardon ~

"Peace Prayer of St. Francis"

Lord, make me an instrument of your peace;

Where there is hatred, let me sow love;

Where there is injury, pardon;

Where there is doubt, faith;

Where there is despair, hope;

Where there is darkness, light;

And where there is sadness, joy.[9]

—AUTHOR UNKNOWN,
circa 1915

---

9. "Peace Prayer of St. Francis, http://www.americancatholic.org/Features/ Francis/peaceprayer.asp. Although very Franciscan in spirit and widely attributed to him, the Peace Prayer of St. Francis was not actually written by Francis of Assisi.

THE PEACE OF ST. FRANCIS, THE PEACE OF CHRIST

Many people, when they think of St. Francis, think of peace; very few people however go deeper. What is the peace which Francis received, experienced and lived, and which he passes on to us? It is the peace of Christ, which is born of the greatest love of all, the love of the cross. It is the peace which the Risen Jesus gave to his disciples when he stood in their midst (cf. Jn 20:19–20).

Franciscan peace is not something saccharine. Hardly! That is not the real St. Francis! Nor is it a kind of pantheistic harmony with forces of the cosmos…That is not Franciscan either! It is not Franciscan, but a notion that some people have invented! The peace of St. Francis is the peace of Christ, and it is found by those who "take up" their "yoke," namely, Christ's commandment:

Love one another as I have loved you (cf. Jn 13:34; 15:12). This yoke cannot be borne with arrogance, presumption or pride, but only with meekness and humbleness of heart.

We turn to you, Francis, and we ask you: Teach us to be "instruments of peace," of that peace which has its source in God, the peace which Jesus has brought us.

HOMILY, ST. FRANCIS SQUARE, ASSISI
FRIDAY, OCTOBER 4, 2013

Pope Francis @Pontifex • September 2, 2013

"We want a peaceful world, we want to be men and women of peace."

LET PEACE BEGIN AT HOME

What is happening in the heart of man? What is happening in the heart of humanity? It is time to stop!

From every corner of the globe, today believers offer up their prayers asking the Lord for the gift of peace and the ability to bring it into every environment. On this first day of the year, may the Lord help us all to set out more decisively on the path of justice and peace. And let us begin at home! Justice and peace at home, among ourselves. It begins at home and then goes out to all humanity. But we have to begin at home. May the Holy Spirit act in hearts, may he melt obstacles and hardness and grant that we may be moved before the weakness of the Baby Jesus. Peace, in fact, requires the strength of meekness, the nonviolent strength of truth and love.

ANGELUS, ST. PETER'S SQUARE,
47TH WORLD DAY OF PEACE
SOLEMNITY OF MARY, MOTHER OF GOD,
WEDNESDAY, JANUARY 1, 2014

Oppose Evil with Good, With Pardon

To love someone who doesn't love us.... It's not easy! Because if we know that a person doesn't like us, then we also tend to bear ill will. But no! We must love even someone who doesn't love us! Opposing evil with good, with pardon, with sharing, with welcome. Thanks to Jesus and to his Spirit, even our life becomes "bread broken" for our brothers. And living like this we discover true joy! The joy of making of oneself a gift, of reciprocating the great gift that we have first received, without merit of our own.

ANGELUS, ST. PETER'S SQUARE
SUNDAY, JUNE 22, 2014

Pope Francis @Pontifex • January 16, 2014

"Let us pray for peace, and let us bring it about, starting in our own homes!"

FACE CONFLICT HEAD ON

Conflict cannot be ignored or concealed. It has to be faced. But if we remain trapped in conflict, we lose our perspective, our horizons shrink and reality itself begins to fall apart. In the midst of conflict, we lose our sense of the profound unity of reality.

When conflict arises, some people simply look at it and go their way as if nothing happened; they wash their hands of it and get on with their lives. Others embrace it in such a way that they become its prisoners; they lose their bearings, project onto institutions their own confusion and dissatisfaction and thus make unity impossible. But there is also a third way, and it is the best way to deal with conflict. It is the willingness to face conflict head on, to resolve it and to make it a link in the chain of a new process. "Blessed are the peacemakers!" (Mt 5:9).

APOSTOLIC EXHORTATION, *EVANGELII GAUDIUM*, 226–227
NOVEMBER 24, 2013

Prerequisites of Lasting Peace

Through the anointing of the Spirit, our human nature is sealed with the holiness of Jesus Christ and we are enabled to love our brothers and sisters with the same love which God has for us. We ought, therefore, to show concrete signs of humility, fraternity, forgiveness and reconciliation. These signs are the prerequisite of a true, stable and lasting peace. Let us ask the Father to anoint us so that we may fully become his children, ever more conformed to Christ, and may learn to see one another as brothers and sisters.

HOMILY, INTERNATIONAL STADIUM, AMMAN, JORDAN
SATURDAY, MAY 24, 2014

Pope Francis @Pontifex • February 18, 2014

"Let us learn from Christ how to pray, to forgive, to sow peace, and to be near those in need."

The Path to Peace

As you know, in the past days I made a pilgrimage to the Holy Land. It was a great gift for the Church, and I thank God for it. He led me through that blessed Land, which saw the historical presence of Jesus and where fundamental events for Judaism, Christianity and Islam took place....

I exhorted the Christian faithful to allow themselves, with open and docile hearts, to be "anointed" by the Holy Spirit, so as to be increasingly capable of acts of humility, fraternity and reconciliation. The Spirit allows one to adopt these attitudes in daily life, with people of various cultures and religions, and thus to become "craftsmen" of peace. Peace is crafted by hand! There are no industries for peace, no. It is fashioned each day, by hand, and also with an open heart so that the gift of God may come. That is why I exhorted the Christian faithful to allow themselves to be "anointed."

GENERAL AUDIENCE, ST. PETER'S SQUARE
WEDNESDAY, MAY 28, 2014

NEVER WAR!

Brothers and sisters, never war! Never war! I think mostly of the children, of those who are deprived of the hope for a dignified life, of a future: dead children, wounded children, maimed children, orphaned children, children who have the remnants of war as toys, children who do not know how to smile. Stop, please! I ask you with all my heart. It is time to stop! Stop, please!

ANGELUS, ST. PETER'S SQUARE
SUNDAY, JULY 27, 2014

Pope Francis @Pontifex • January 18, 2014

"Wars shatter so many lives. I think especially of children robbed of their childhood."

DISCOVER YOUR BROTHER OR SISTER

I appeal forcefully to all those who sow violence and death by force of arms: in the person you today see simply as an enemy to be beaten, discover rather your brother or sister, and hold back your hand! Give up the way of arms and go out to meet the other in dialogue, pardon and reconciliation, in order to rebuild justice, trust, and hope around you!

MESSAGE FOR 2014 WORLD DAY OF PEACE,
FROM THE VATICAN
SUNDAY, DECEMBER 8, 2013

A CULTURE OF ENCOUNTER AND OUTREACH

Being closed and isolated always makes for a stifling, heavy atmosphere which sooner or later ends up creating sadness and oppression. What is needed instead is a shared commitment to favoring a culture of encounter, for only those able to reach out to others are capable of bearing fruit, creating bonds of communion, radiating joy and being peacemakers.

The scenes of destruction and death which we have witnessed in the past year confirm all this—if ever we needed such confirmation. How much pain and desperation are caused by self-centeredness which gradually takes the form of envy, selfishness, competition and the thirst for power and money! At times it seems that these realities are destined to have the upper hand. Christmas, on the other hand, inspires in us Christians the certainty that the final, definitive word belongs to the Prince of Peace, who changes "swords into plowshares and spears into pruning hooks" (cf. Is 2:4), transforming selfishness into self-giving and revenge into forgiveness.

ADDRESS TO THE MEMBERS OF THE DIPLOMATIC CORPS,
SALA REGIA
MONDAY, JANUARY 13, 2014

Pope Francis @Pontifex • June 6, 2014

"Peace is a gift of God, but requires our efforts. Let us be people of peace in prayer and deed. #weprayforpeace"

THE HEROISM THAT LEADS TO PEACE AND JUSTICE

At the heart of every authentic dialogue there is, first and foremost, recognition and respect for the other. There is, above all, the "heroism" of forgiveness and mercy, which frees us from resentment and hate, and which opens a truly new path. It is a long and difficult path, which requires patience and courage, but it is the only one that can lead to peace and justice. For the good of all the people and for the future of your children, I call upon you to have this courage.

MESSAGE FOR THE VENEZUELAN GOVERNMENT AND THE OPPOSITION, FROM THE VATICAN
THURSDAY, APRIL 10, 2014

CULTIVATE THE PLANT OF PEACE

Those who would cultivate the plant of peace must never forget that God alone gives the growth. True peace, the peace which the world cannot give, is a gift to us from Jesus Christ. For all the grievous attacks it endures today, peace can always flourish again. I thank you, always, because you continue to "make peace grow" through charity, which is the ultimate aim of all your organizations. With unity and charity Christ's disciples strive to be peacemakers everywhere, in all peoples and communities, and to overcome persistent forms of discrimination, starting with those based on religion.

ADDRESS TO MEMBERS OF THE AID AGENCIES FOR THE
ORIENTAL CHURCHES, CLEMENTINE HALL
THURSDAY, JUNE 26, 2014

INSTRUMENTS AND ARTISANS OF PEACE

In this, the birthplace of the Prince of Peace, I wish to invite you, President Mahmoud Abbas, together with President Shimon Peres, to join me in heartfelt prayer to God for the gift of peace. I offer my home in the Vatican as a place for this encounter of prayer.

All of us want peace. Many people build it day by day through small gestures and acts; many of them are suffering, yet patiently persevere in their efforts to be peacemakers. All of us—especially those placed at the service of their respective peoples—have the duty to become instruments and artisans of peace, especially by our prayers.

Building peace is difficult, but living without peace is a constant torment. The men and women of these lands, and of the entire world, all of them, ask us to bring before God their fervent hopes for peace.

REGINA CAELI, BETHLEHEM
SUNDAY, MAY 25, 2014

LET US SOW LOVE, PARDON, AND UNITY

Let us ask the Lord: Lord, grant that we be more and more united, never to be instruments of division; enable us to commit ourselves, as the beautiful Franciscan prayer says, to sowing love where there is hatred; where there is injury, pardon; and unity where there is discord. So be it.

GENERAL AUDIENCE, ST. PETER'S SQUARE
WEDNESDAY, SEPTEMBER 25, 2013

MAY GOD CHANGE THE HEARTS OF THE VIOLENT

May God change the hearts of the violent. May God change the hearts of those who seek war. May God change the hearts of those who manufacture and sell arms and may he strengthen the hearts and minds of peacemakers and grant them every blessing. May God bless you all!

ADDRESS TO REFUGEES AND DISABLED YOUNG PEOPLE,
LATIN CHURCH, BETHANY BEYOND THE JORDAN
SATURDAY, MAY 24, 2014

Pope Francis @Pontifex • September 3, 2013

"With utmost firmness I condemn the use of chemical weapons."

THE COMMON GOOD AND PEACE IN SOCIETY

Peace in society cannot be understood as pacification or the mere absence of violence resulting from the domination of one part of society over others. Nor does true peace act as a pretext for justifying a social structure which silences or appeases the poor, so that the more affluent can placidly support their lifestyle while others have to make do as they can. Demands involving the distribution of wealth, concern for the poor and human rights cannot be suppressed under the guise of creating a consensus on paper or a transient peace for a contented minority. The dignity of the human person and the common good rank higher than the comfort of those who refuse to renounce their privileges. When these values are threatened, a prophetic voice must be raised.

APOSTOLIC EXHORTATION,
EVANGELII GAUDIUM, 218
NOVEMBER 24, 2013

Pope Francis @Pontifex • August 9, 2014

"Violence is not conquered by violence. Lord, send us the gift of peace. #prayforpeace"

In War, All Is Lost

Tomorrow is the 100ᵀᴴ anniversary of the start of World War I, which had millions of victims and caused immense devastation. This conflict, which Pope Benedict XVI called a "senseless slaughter," resolved after four long years into a most fragile peace. Tomorrow will be a day of mourning in memory of this tragedy. While remembering this tragic event, I hope that the mistakes of the past are not repeated, that the lessons of history are acknowledged, and that the causes for peace may always prevail through patient and courageous dialogue....

Let us remember that in war all is lost and in peace nothing.

ANGELUS, ST. PETER'S SQUARE
SUNDAY, JULY 27, 2014

True Peace is Not a "Façade"

True peace—we know this well—is not a balance of opposing forces. It is not a lovely "façade" which conceals conflicts and divisions. Peace calls for daily commitment, but making peace is an art, starting from God's gift, from the grace which he has given us in Jesus Christ.

Looking at the Child in the manger, Child of peace, our thoughts turn to those children who are the most vulnerable victims of wars, but we think too of the elderly, to battered women, to the sick… Wars shatter and hurt so many lives!

URBI ET ORBI, LOGGIA OF ST. PETER'S BASILICA
CHRISTMAS, DECEMBER 25, 2013

Pope Francis @Pontifex • September 6, 2013
"All men and women of good will are bound by the task of pursuing peace. #prayforpeace"

A Prayer for Peace

Our world is a legacy bequeathed to us from past generations, but it is also on loan to us from our children: our children who are weary, worn out by conflicts and yearning for the dawn of peace, our children who plead with us to tear down the walls of enmity and to set out on the path of dialogue and peace, so that love and friendship will prevail.

Many, all too many, of those children have been innocent victims of war and violence, saplings cut down at the height of their promise. It is our duty to ensure that their sacrifice is not in vain. The memory of these children instills in us the courage of peace, the strength to persevere undaunted in dialogue, the patience to weave, day by day, an ever more robust fabric of respectful and peaceful coexistence, for the glory of God and the good of all....

We have tried so many times and over so many years to resolve our conflicts by our own powers and by the force of our arms. How many moments of hostility and darkness have we experienced; how much blood has been shed; how many lives have been shattered; how many hopes have been buried... But our efforts have been in vain.

Now, Lord, come to our aid! Grant us peace, teach us peace; guide our steps in the way of peace. Open our eyes and our hearts, and give us the courage to say: "Never again war!"; "With war everything is lost." Instill in our hearts the courage to take concrete steps to achieve peace.

Lord, God of Abraham, God of the Prophets, God of Love, you created us and you call us to live as brothers and sisters. Give us the strength daily to be instruments of peace; enable us to see everyone who crosses our path as our brother or sister. Make us sensitive to the plea of our citizens who entreat us to turn our weapons of war into implements of peace, our trepidation into confident trust, and our quarreling into forgiveness.

Keep alive within us the flame of hope, so that with patience and perseverance we may opt for dialogue and reconciliation. In this way may peace triumph at last, and may the words "division," "hatred" and "war" be banished from the heart of every man and woman. Lord, defuse the violence of our tongues and our hands. Renew our hearts and minds, so that the word which always brings us together will be "brother," and our way of life will always be that of: Shalom, Peace, Salaam!

Amen.

INVOCATION FOR PEACE, VATICAN GARDENS
SUNDAY, JUNE 8, 2014

CHAPTER TEN

~ Respect and Protect Creation ~

The Canticle of Creation

All praise be yours, my Lord, through all that you
   have made,

And first my lord Brother Sun,

Who brings the day; and light you give to us
   through him.

How beautiful is he, how radiant in all his
   splendor!

Of you, Most High, he bears the likeness.

All praise be yours, my Lord, through Sister
   Moon and Stars;

In the heavens you have made them, bright

And precious and fair.[10]

10. "The Canticle of Brother Sun," *Omnibus*, pp. 130–131.

St. Francis's Witness

Francis began the Canticle of the Creatures with these words:"Praised may you be, Most High, All-powerful God, good Lord...by all your creatures." Love for all creation, for its harmony. St. Francis of Assisi bears witness to the need to respect all that God has created and as he created it, without manipulating and destroying creation; rather to help it grow, to become more beautiful and more like what God created it to be. And above all, St. Francis witnesses to respect for everyone, he testifies that each of us is called to protect our neighbor, that the human person is at the center of creation, at the place where God—our creator— willed that we should be. Not at the mercy of the idols we have created! Harmony and peace! Francis was a man of harmony and peace. From this City of Peace, I repeat with all the strength and the meekness of love: Let us respect creation, let us not be instruments of destruction!

HOMILY, ST. FRANCIS SQUARE, ASSISI
FRIDAY, OCTOBER 4, 2013

The Gift of Nature

The human family has received from the Creator a common gift: nature. The Christian view of creation includes a positive judgment about the legitimacy of interventions on nature if these are meant to be beneficial and are performed responsibly, that is to say, by acknowledging the "grammar" inscribed in nature and by wisely using resources for the benefit of all, with respect for the beauty, finality and usefulness of every living being and its place in the ecosystem.

Nature, in a word, is at our disposition and we are called to exercise a responsible stewardship over it. Yet so often we are driven by greed and by the arrogance of dominion, possession, manipulation and exploitation; we do not preserve nature; nor do we respect it or consider it a gracious gift which we must care for and set at the service of our brothers and sisters, including future generations.

MESSAGE FOR 2014 WORLD DAY OF PEACE,
FROM THE VATICAN
SUNDAY, DECEMBER 8, 2013

Pope Francis @Pontifex • March 19, 2013

"Let us keep a place for Christ in our lives, let us care for one another and let us be loving custodians of creation."

OUR TRUE TREASURE

When a person discovers God, the true treasure, he abandons a selfish lifestyle and seeks to share with others the charity which comes from God. He who becomes a friend of God, loves his brothers and sisters, commits himself to safeguarding their life and their health, and also to respecting the environment and nature.

HOMILY, PARK OF THE ROYAL PALACE OF CASERTA
SATURDAY, JULY 26, 2014

SAFEGUARD CREATION FOR FUTURE GENERATIONS

Work must be combined with the preservation of creation so that this may be responsibly safeguarded for future generations. Creation is not a good to be exploited but a gift to look after. Ecological commitment itself affords an opportunity for new concern in the sectors linked to it, such as energy, and the prevention and removal of different forms of pollution, being alert to forest fires in the wooded land that is your patrimony, and so forth. May caring for creation, and looking after man through dignified work be a common task! Ecology…and also "human" ecology"!

ADDRESS TO THE WORKERS OF LARGO CARLO FELICE,
CAGLIARI
SUNDAY, SEPTEMBER 22, 2013

Pope Francis @Pontifex • November 14, 2013

"Take care of God's creation. But above all, take care of people in need."

CONTEMPLATE THE GOODNESS OF CREATION

In the first Chapter of Genesis, right at the beginning of the Bible, what is emphasized is that God is pleased with his creation, stressing repeatedly the beauty and goodness of every single thing. At the end of each day, it is written: "God saw that it was good" (1:12, 18, 21, 25). If God sees creation as good, as a beautiful thing, then we too must take this attitude and see that creation is a good and beautiful thing. Now, this is the gift of knowledge that allows us to see this beauty, therefore we praise God, giving thanks to him for having granted us so much beauty. And when God finished creating man he didn't say "he saw that this was good," but said that this was "very good" (v. 31). In the eyes of God we are the most beautiful thing, the greatest, the best of creation: even the Angels are beneath us, we are more than the angels, as we heard in the Book of Psalms. The Lord favors us!...

All this is a source of serenity and peace and makes the Christian a joyful witness of God, in the footsteps of St. Francis of Assisi and so many saints who knew how to praise and laud his love through the contemplation of creation.

GENERAL AUDIENCE, ST. PETER'S SQUARE
WEDNESDAY, MAY 21, 2014

Protect One Another and the Environment

I would like to ask all those who have positions of responsibility in economic, political and social life, and all men and women of goodwill: let us be "protectors" of creation, protectors of God's plan inscribed in nature, protectors of one another and of the environment. Let us not allow omens of destruction and death to accompany the advance of this world! But to be "protectors," we also have to keep watch over ourselves! Let us not forget that hatred, envy and pride defile our lives! Being protectors, then, also means keeping watch over our emotions, over our hearts, because they are the seat of good and evil intentions: intentions that build up and tear down! We must not be afraid of goodness or even tenderness!

HOMILY, ST. PETER'S SQUARE, MASS FOR THE
INAUGURATION OF THE PONTIFICATE
SOLEMNITY OF SAINT JOSEPH,
TUESDAY, MARCH 19, 2013

If We Destroy Creation, Creation Will Destroy Us! Creation is not some possession that we can lord over for our own pleasure; nor, even less, is it the property of only some people, the few: creation is a gift, it is the marvelous gift that God has given us, so that we will take care of it and harness it for the benefit of all, always with great respect and gratitude....

We must protect creation for it is a gift which the Lord has given us, it is God's present to us; we are the guardians of creation. When we exploit creation, we destroy that sign of God's love. To destroy creation is to say to God: "I don't care." And this is not good: this is sin.

Custody of creation is precisely custody of God's gift and it is saying to God: "thank you, I am the guardian of creation so as to make it progress, never to destroy your gift." This must be our attitude to creation: guard it for if we destroy creation, creation will destroy us!

GENERAL AUDIENCE, ST. PETER'S SQUARE
WEDNESDAY, MAY 21, 2014

The Earth is Our Common Home

An authentic faith—which is never comfortable or completely personal—always involves a deep desire to change the world, to transmit values, to leave this earth somehow better that we found it. We love this magnificent planet on which God has put us, and we love the human family which dwells here, with all its tragedies and struggles, its hopes and aspirations, its strengths and weaknesses. The earth is our common home and all of us are brothers and sisters.

APOSTOLIC EXHORTATION, *EVANGELII GAUDIUM*, 183
NOVEMBER 24, 2013

Pope Francis @Pontifex • June 5, 2013
"Care of creation is not just something God spoke of at the dawn of history: he entrusts it to each of us as part of his plan."

THE DISGRACE OF WORLD HUNGER

In a particular way, the agricultural sector is the primary productive sector with the crucial vocation of cultivating and protecting natural resources in order to feed humanity. In this regard the continuing disgrace of hunger in the world moves me to share with you the question: How are we using the earth's resources? Contemporary societies should reflect on the hierarchy of priorities to which production is directed. It is a truly pressing duty to use the earth's resources in such a way that all may be free from hunger. Initiatives and possible solutions are many, and are not limited to an increase in production. It is well known that present production is sufficient, and yet millions of persons continue to suffer and die from hunger, and this is a real scandal. We need, then, to find ways by which all may benefit from the fruits of the earth, not only to avoid the widening gap between those who have more and those who must be content with the crumbs, but above all because it is a question of justice, equality and respect for every human being.

MESSAGE FOR 2014 WORLD DAY OF PEACE,
FROM THE VATICAN
SUNDAY, DECEMBER 8, 2013

The Stewardship of Creation

It is our profound conviction that the future of the human family depends also on how we safeguard—both prudently and compassionately, with justice and fairness—the gift of creation that our Creator has entrusted to us. Therefore, we acknowledge in repentance the wrongful mistreatment of our planet, which is tantamount to sin before the eyes of God. We reaffirm our responsibility and obligation to foster a sense of humility and moderation so that all may feel the need to respect creation and to safeguard it with care. Together, we pledge our commitment to raising awareness about the stewardship of creation; we appeal to all people of goodwill to consider ways of living less wastefully and more frugally, manifesting less greed and more generosity for the protection of God's world and the benefit of His people.

COMMON DECLARATION OF POPE FRANCIS AND THE ECUMENICAL PATRIARCH BARTHOLOMEW I, JERUSALEM SUNDAY, MAY 25, 2014

LET US PROTECT ALL CREATION!

This is the invitation which I address to everyone: Let us accept the grace of Christ's Resurrection! Let us be renewed by God's mercy, let us be loved by Jesus, let us enable the power of his love to transform our lives too; and let us become agents of this mercy, channels through which God can water the earth, protect all creation and make justice and peace flourish.

URBI ET ORBI, LOGGIA OF ST. PETER'S BASILICA
EASTER SUNDAY, MARCH 31, 2013

About the Author

Pope Francis, formerly Cardinal Jorge Mario Bergoglio, S.J., served the Jesuits as novice master, lecturer, provincial, confessor, and spiritual director before Pope John Paul II named him Archbishop of Buenos Aires. He was elected to the papacy on March 13, 2013. He is the first pope from the Americas and the first pope to choose the name Francis, in honor of St. Francis of Assisi.

~ ~ ~

About the Editor

Alicia (Ramírez de Arellano) von Stamwitz was born in Cuba and immigrated to the United Sates in 1960. She is an award-winning freelance author and longtime editor with the religious press. Her interviews and profiles of today's most influential spiritual leaders are published internationally. She lives in Missouri with her family. More information can be found at www.aliciavonstamwitz.com.